P
Preparatory signal in Starting System 1.

↑ •

S No later than the warning signal: Sa the short course.

At a rounding or finishing *mark*: *Finish* between the nearby *mark* and this boat.

↑ ••

C000061573

↑↓•

Z Rule 30.2 is in effect. (Removed with one long sound 1 minute before the starting signal.)

↑••↓•

First Substitute General recall. The preparatory signal (with the class flag in Starting System 1) will be made 1 minute after removal.

Black flag	↑↓•	Rule 30.3 is in effect. (Removed with one long sound 1 minute before the starting signal.)
Blue flag or shape	↑•	Preparatory signal in Starting System 2.
	(no sound)	At the finishing line: This race committee boat is in position at the finishing line.
Red flag or shape	↑•	Starting signal in Starting System 2.
Yellow flag or shape	↑•	Warning signal in Starting System 2.

↑••↓•

↑••↓•

↑••↓•

↑••↓•

↑••↓•

↑••↓•

Numeral pennants 1–6. Used with AP

THE
RACING RULES
OF
SAILING

for 1997–2000

**Including the
RYA Prescriptions**

Royal Yachting Association
RYA House, Romsey Road
Eastleigh, Hampshire SO50 9YA
Telephone: 01703 627400
Fax: 01703 629924
E-Mail: admin@rya.org.uk

The Racing Rules of Sailing take effect from 1 April 1997:
the RYA prescribes that events beginning on or after 15 March
1997 may use the 1997-2000 RRS; events ending on or before
3 April 1997 may use the 1993-96 IYRR.

Published by the Royal Yachting Association
RYA House, Romsey Road, Eastleigh SO50 9YA.

© 1997 International Sailing Federation

© 1997 Royal Yachting Association

CONTENTS

SPORTSMANSHIP AND THE RULES

Competitors in the sport of sailing are governed by a body of rules that they are expected to follow and enforce. A fundamental principle of sportsmanship is that when competitors break a rule they will promptly take a penalty or retire.

INTRODUCTION

The Racing Rules of Sailing includes two main sections. The first, Parts 1-7, contains rules that affect all competitors. The second section contains appendices that provide details of rules, rules that apply to particular kinds of racing, and rules that affect only a small number of competitors or officials.

The racing rules are revised and published every four years by the International Sailing Federation (ISAF), the international authority for the sport. This edition becomes effective on 1 April 1997. No changes are contemplated before 2001, but changes determined by the ISAF to be urgent will be made as needed and announced through national authorities.

Terminology A term used in the sense stated in the Definitions is printed in italics or, in preambles, in bold italics (for example, *racing* and ***racing***). Other words and terms are used in the sense ordinarily understood in nautical or general use. 'Race committee' includes any person or committee performing a race committee function. 'Class rules' includes rules of handicapping and rating systems.

Appendices When the rules of an appendix apply, they take precedence over any conflicting rules in Parts 1-7. A reference to a rule of an appendix will contain the letter of the appendix and the rule number; for example, 'rule A1.1'. (There is no Appendix I or Appendix O.)

Changes to the Rules The prescriptions of a national authority, class rules or the sailing instructions may change a racing rule only as permitted in rule 86.

RYA Precriptions to the racing rules are printed on separate pages, coloured yellow. A rule prescribed to is marked with a dagger (†) in the margin.

PART 1 – FUNDAMENTAL RULES

1   SAFETY

1.1   Helping Those in Danger

A boat or competitor shall give all possible help to any person or vessel in danger.

1.2   Life-Saving Equipment and Personal Buoyancy

A boat shall carry adequate life-saving equipment for all persons on board, including one item ready for immediate use, unless her class rules make some other provision. Each competitor is individually responsible for wearing personal buoyancy adequate for the conditions.

2   FAIR SAILING

A boat and her owner shall compete in compliance with recognized principles of sportsmanship and fair play. A boat may be penalized under this rule only if it is clearly established that these principles have been violated.

3   ACCEPTANCE OF THE RULES

By participating in a race conducted under these racing rules, each competitor and boat owner agrees

(a)   to be governed by the *rules*;

(b)   to accept the penalties imposed and other action taken under the *rules*, subject to the appeal and review procedures provided in them, as the final determination of any matter arising under the *rules*; and

(c)   with respect to such determination, not to resort to any court or other tribunal not provided by the *rules*.

4   DECISION TO RACE

A boat is solely responsible for deciding whether or not to *start* or to continue *racing*.

5   DRUGS

A competitor shall neither take a substance nor use a method banned by Appendix L. An alleged breach of this rule shall not be grounds for a *protest*, and rule 63.1 does not apply.

4

PART 2 – WHEN BOATS MEET

*The rules of Part 2 apply between boats that are sailing in or near the racing area and intend to **race**, are **racing**, or have been **racing**. However, a boat not **racing** shall not be penalized for breaking one of these rules, except rule 22.1. The International Regulations for Preventing Collisions at Sea or government right-of-way rules apply between a boat sailing under these rules and a vessel that is not, and they replace these rules if the sailing instructions so state.*

Section A – Right of Way

*A boat has right of way when another boat is required to **keep clear** of her. However, some rules in Sections B and C limit the actions of a right-of-way boat.*

10   ON OPPOSITE TACKS

When boats are on opposite *tacks*, a *port-tack* boat shall *keep clear* of a *starboard-tack* boat.

11   ON THE SAME TACK, OVERLAPPED

When boats are on the same *tack* and *overlapped*, a *windward* boat shall *keep clear* of a *leeward* boat.

12   ON THE SAME TACK, NOT OVERLAPPED

When boats are on the same *tack* and not *overlapped*, a boat *clear astern* shall *keep clear* of a boat *clear ahead*.

13   WHILE TACKING

After a boat passes head to wind, she shall *keep clear* of other boats until she is on a close-hauled course. During that time rules 10, 11 and 12 do not apply. If two boats are subject to this rule at the same time, the one on the other's port side shall *keep clear*.

Section B – General Limitations

14   AVOIDING CONTACT

A boat shall avoid contact with another boat if reasonably possible. However, a right-of-way boat or one entitled to *room*

(a)   need not act to avoid contact until it is clear that the other boat is not *keeping clear* or giving *room*, and

(b)   **(b)   shall not be penalized under this rule unless there is contact that causes damage.**

15   ACQUIRING RIGHT OF WAY

When a boat acquires right of way, she shall initially give the other boat *room* to *keep clear*, unless she acquires right of way because of the other boat's actions.

16   CHANGING COURSE

When a right-of-way boat changes course, she shall give the other boat *room* to *keep clear*.

17   ON THE SAME TACK; PROPER COURSE

17.1   A boat *clear astern* that becomes *overlapped* to *leeward* and within two of her hull lengths of a *windward* boat shall not sail above her *proper course* while the boats remain *overlapped* and less than that distance apart, unless as a result she falls astern of the *windward* boat.

17.2   Except on a beat to windward, while a boat is less than two of her hull lengths from a *leeward* boat or a boat *clear astern* steering a course to *leeward* of her, she shall not sail below her *proper course* unless she gybes.

Section C – At Marks and Obstructions

When a Section C rule applies, the rules in Sections A and B continue to apply unless the Section C rule modifies them or states that they do not apply.

18   PASSING MARKS AND OBSTRUCTIONS

18.1   When this Rule Applies

Rule 18 applies at a *mark* or *obstruction* to be left on the same side when boats are about to pass it until they have passed it. However, it does not apply

(a)   at a starting *mark* or its anchor line surrounded by navigable water from the time the boats are approaching them to *start* until they have passed them, or

(b)   between boats on opposite *tacks* when they are on a beat to windward or when the *proper course* for one of them to pass the *mark* or *obstruction* is to tack.

18.2   Giving Room; Keeping Clear

(a)   When boats are *overlapped* before one of them reaches the *two-length zone*, if the outside boat has right of way she shall give the inside boat *room* to pass the *mark* or *obstruction*, or if the inside boat has right of way the outside boat shall *keep clear*. If they are still *overlapped* when one of them reaches the *two-length zone*, the outside boat's obligation continues even if the *overlap* is broken later. This rule does not apply if the outside boat is unable to give *room* when the *overlap* begins.

(b)   If a boat is *clear ahead* when she reaches the *two-length zone*, the boat *clear astern* shall *keep clear* even if an *overlap* is established later. Rule 10 does not apply. If the boat *clear ahead* tacks, rule 13 applies and this rule no longer does.

(c)   If there is reasonable doubt that a boat established or broke an *overlap* in time, it shall be presumed that she did not.

18.3   Tacking

If two boats were on opposite *tacks* and one of them tacked within the *two-length zone* to pass a *mark* or *obstruction*, rule 18.2 does not apply. The boat that tacked

(a)   shall not cause the other boat to sail above close-hauled to avoid her or prevent the other boat from passing the *mark* or *obstruction*, and

(b)   shall *keep clear* if the other boat becomes *overlapped* inside her, in which case rule 15 does not apply.

18.4   Gybing

When rule 18.2(a) applies and an inside *overlapped* right-of-way boat must gybe at the *mark* or *obstruction* to sail her *proper course*, she shall pass no farther from the *mark* or *obstruction* than needed to sail that course.

18.5   Passing a Continuing Obstruction

At a continuing *obstruction*, rule 18.2 is modified so that while boats are passing the *obstruction* an outside boat's obligation ends if the *overlap* is broken, and a boat *clear astern* may establish an inside *overlap* provided there is room at that time to pass between the other boat and the *obstruction*. If she does so, her obligation under rule 18.2(b) ends.

19   ROOM TO TACK AT AN OBSTRUCTION

19.1   When safety requires a close-hauled boat to make a substantial course change to avoid an *obstruction* and she intends to tack, but cannot tack and avoid another boat on the same *tack*, she shall hail for *room* to do so. Before tacking she shall give the hailed boat time to respond. The hailed boat shall either

(a)   tack as soon as possible, in which case the hailing boat shall also tack as soon as possible, or

(b)   immediately reply 'You tack', in which case the hailing boat shall immediately tack and the hailed boat shall give *room*, and rules 10 and 13 do not apply.

19.2   Rule 19.1 does not apply at a starting *mark* or its anchor line surrounded by navigable water from the time boats are approaching them to *start* until they have passed them or at a *mark* that the hailed boat can fetch. When rule 19.1 applies, rule 18 does not.

Section D – Other Rules

When rule 20 or 21 applies between two boats, Section A rules do not.

20   STARTING ERRORS; PENALTY TURNS; MOVING ASTERN

A boat sailing towards the pre-start side of the starting line or its extensions to comply with rule 29.1 or rule 30.1 shall *keep clear* of a boat not doing so until she is completely on the pre-start side. A boat making penalty turns shall *keep clear* of one that is not. A boat moving astern by backing a sail shall *keep clear* of one that is not.

21   CAPSIZED, ANCHORED OR AGROUND; RESCUING

If possible, a boat shall avoid a boat that is capsized or has not regained control after capsizing, is anchored or aground, or is trying to help a person or vessel in danger. A boat is capsized when her masthead is in the water.

22   INTERFERING WITH ANOTHER BOAT

22.1   If reasonably possible, a boat not *racing* shall not interfere with a boat that is *racing*.

22.2   A boat shall not deliberately interfere with a boat making penalty turns to delay her.

PART 3 – CONDUCT OF A RACE

25   SAILING INSTRUCTIONS AND SIGNALS

Sailing instructions shall be made available to each boat before a race begins. The race committee shall conduct the race using the visual and sound signals defined in the Race Signals and any other signals included in the sailing instructions.

26   STARTING SYSTEMS 1 AND 2

26.1   A race shall be started by using either System 1 or System 2. Signals shall be made at five-minute intervals. Times shall be taken from the visual signals; the failure of a sound signal shall be disregarded. Signals shall be as follows (flags of a single colour may be replaced by shapes of the same colour):

Signal	System 1	System 2
Warning	Class flag, 1 sound	Yellow flag, 1 sound
Preparatory	Flag P, 1 sound	Blue flag, 1 sound
Starting	Flags removed, 1 sound	Red flag, 1 sound

26.2   In System 1, when classes are started at ten-minute intervals, the warning signal for each succeeding class shall be displayed at the starting signal of the preceding class. When five-minute intervals are used, flag P shall be left displayed until the last class starts and the warning signal for each succeeding class shall be displayed at the time of the preparatory signal of the preceding class. If there is a general recall, the warning and preparatory signals of any succeeding classes shall be removed immediately after the general recall has been signalled.

26.3   In System 2, each signal shall be removed one minute before the next is made. When classes are started at ten-minute intervals, the starting signal for each class shall be the warning signal for the next.

When classes are started at five-minute intervals, the preparatory signal for each class shall be the warning signal for the next. When class flags are used, they shall be displayed before or with the preparatory signal for the class.

27   OTHER RACE COMMITTEE ACTIONS BEFORE THE STARTING SIGNAL

27.1   No later than the warning signal, the race committee shall signal or otherwise designate the course to be sailed if the sailing instructions have not stated the course, and it may replace one course signal with another, signal that a designated short course will be used (flag S), and apply rule 40 (flag Y).

27.2   No later than the preparatory signal, the race committee may move a starting *mark* and may apply rule 30.

27.3   Before the starting signal, the race committee may *postpone* (flag AP) or *abandon* the race (flag N over H or A) for any reason.

28   SAILING THE COURSE

28.1   A boat shall *start*, pass each *mark* on the required side in the correct order, and *finish*, so that a string representing her wake after *starting* and until *finishing* would, when drawn taut, lie on the required side of each *mark* and touch each rounding *mark*. She may correct any errors to comply with this rule, provided she has not already *finished*. After *finishing*, a boat need not cross the finishing line completely.

28.2   A *mark* has a required side for a boat only when she is on a leg that the *mark* begins, bounds or ends, except that a starting mark begins to have a required side when she is approaching the starting line from its pre-start side to *start*.

29   STARTING; RECALLS

29.1   **On the Course Side at the Start**

When at her starting signal any part of a boat's hull, crew or equipment is on the course side of the starting line, the boat shall sail completely to the pre-start side of the line before *starting*.

29.2   Individual Recall

When at her starting signal a boat must comply with rule 29.1 or rule 30.1, the race committee shall promptly display flag X. The signal shall be displayed until all such boats are completely on the pre-start side of the starting line or its extensions and have complied with rule 30.1 if it applies, but not later than four minutes after the starting signal or one minute before any later starting signal, whichever is earlier.

29.3   General Recall

When at the starting signal several unidentified boats are on the course side of the starting line or there has been an error in the starting procedure, the race committee may signal a general recall (flag First Substitute). The preparatory signal for a new start for the recalled class shall be made one minute after the First Substitute is lowered, and the starts for any succeeding classes shall follow the new start.

30   STARTING PENALTIES

30.1   I Flag Rule

If flag I has been displayed before or with her preparatory signal, and any part of a boat's hull, crew or equipment is on the course side of the starting line or its extensions during the minute before her starting signal, she shall sail to the pre-start side of the line around either end before *starting*.

30.2   Z Flag Rule

If flag Z has been displayed before or with her preparatory signal, and any part of a boat's hull, crew or equipment is identified within the triangle formed by the ends of the starting line and the first *mark* during the minute before her starting signal and a general recall is then signalled, she shall, without a hearing, be given a 20% scoring penalty calculated as stated in rule 44.3(c). If the race is restarted, resailed or rescheduled, she shall still be given the penalty.

30.3   Black Flag Rule

If a black flag has been displayed before or with her preparatory signal, and any part of a boat's hull, crew or equipment is identified within the triangle formed by the ends of the starting line and the first *mark* during the minute before her starting signal, the boat will be disqualified without a hearing. If the race is restarted, resailed or rescheduled, she is not entitled to compete in it. If a general recall is signalled or the race is *abandoned*, the race committee shall display her sail number.

31   TOUCHING A MARK

31.1   While *racing*, a boat shall not touch a starting *mark* before *starting*, a *mark* that begins, bounds or ends the leg of the course on which she is sailing, or a finishing *mark* after *finishing*.

31.2   A boat that has broken rule 31.1 may, after getting well clear of other boats as soon as possible, take a penalty by promptly making one complete 360° turn including one tack and one gybe. When a boat takes the penalty after touching a finishing *mark*, she shall return completely to the course side of the line before *finishing*. However, if a boat has gained a significant advantage in the race or series by touching the *mark* she shall retire.

31.3   When a boat is wrongfully compelled by another boat to break rule 31.1, she shall be exonerated

   (a)   if the other boat acknowledges breaking a rule of Part 2 by taking a penalty or retiring immediately, or

   (b)   under rule 64.1(b), after successfully protesting another boat involved in the same incident.

32   SHORTENING OR ABANDONING AFTER THE START

After the starting signal, the race committee may *abandon* the race (flag N or flag N over H or A) or shorten the course (flag S), as appropriate,

   (a)   because of an error in the starting procedure,

   (b)   because of foul weather,

   (c)   because of insufficient wind making it unlikely that any boat will *finish* within the time limit,

(d)   because a *mark* is missing or out of position, or

(e)   for any other reason directly affecting the safety or fairness of the competition.

However, after one boat has sailed the course and *finished* within the time limit, if any, the race committee shall not *abandon* the race without considering the consequences for all boats in the race or series.

33   CHANGING THE COURSE AFTER THE START

At any rounding *mark* the race committee may signal a change of the direction of the next leg of the course by displaying flag C and the compass bearing of that leg before any boat begins it. The race committee may change the length of the next leg by displaying flag C and a '−' if the leg will be shortened or a '+' if the leg will be lengthened.

34   MARK MISSING

When a *mark* is missing or out of position, the race committee shall, if possible,

(a)   replace it in its correct position, or

(b)   substitute one of similar appearance, or a buoy or vessel displaying flag M.

35   TIME LIMIT

If one boat sails the course as required in rule 28.1 and *finishes* within the time limit, if any, all boats shall be scored unless the race is *abandoned*. If no boat *finishes* within the time limit, the race committee shall *abandon* the race.

36   RACES TO BE RESTARTED OR RESAILED

If a race is restarted or resailed, a breach of a *rule*, other than rule 30.3, in the original race shall not prohibit a boat from competing or, except under rule 30.2, 30.3 or 69, cause her to be penalized.

PART 4 – OTHER REQUIREMENTS WHEN RACING

*Part 4 rules apply only to boats **racing**.*

40 PERSONAL BUOYANCY

When flag Y is displayed before or with the warning signal, competitors shall wear life-jackets or other adequate personal buoyancy. Wet suits and dry suits are not adequate personal buoyancy.

41 OUTSIDE HELP

A boat may receive outside help as provided for in rule 1. Otherwise, she shall not receive help except for an ill or injured crew member or, after a collision, from the crew of the other boat.

42 PROPULSION

42.1 Basic Rule

Except when permitted in rule 42.3 or rule 45, a boat shall compete by using only the wind and water to increase, maintain or decrease her speed. Her crew may adjust the trim of sails and hull, and perform other acts of seamanship, but shall not otherwise move their bodies to propel the boat.

42.2 Prohibited Actions

Without limiting the application of rule 42.1, these actions are prohibited:

(a) pumping: repeated fanning of any sail either by trimming and releasing the sail or by vertical or athwartships body movement;

(b) rocking: repeated rolling of the boat, induced either by body movement or adjustment of the sails or centreboard, that does not facilitate steering;

(c)   ooching: sudden forward body movement, stopped abruptly;

(d)   sculling: repeated movement of the helm not necessary for steering;

(e)   repeated tacks or gybes unrelated to changes in the wind or to tactical considerations.

42.3   Exceptions

(a)   A boat's crew may move their bodies to exaggerate the rolling that facilitates steering the boat through a tack or a gybe, provided that, just after the tack or gybe is completed, the boat's speed is not greater than it would have been in the absence of the tack or gybe.

(b)   Except on a beat to windward, when surfing (rapidly accelerating down the leeward side of a wave) or planing is possible, the boat's crew may pull the sheet and the guy controlling any sail in order to initiate surfing or planing, but only once for each wave or gust of wind.

(c)   Any means of propulsion may be used to help a person or another vessel in danger.

(d)   To get clear after grounding or colliding with another boat or object, a boat may use force applied by the crew of either boat and any equipment other than a propulsion engine.

43   COMPETITOR CLOTHING AND EQUIPMENT

43.1

(a)   Competitors shall not wear or carry clothing or equipment for the purpose of increasing their weight.

(b)   Furthermore, a competitor's clothing and equipment shall not weigh more than 8 kilograms, excluding a hiking or trapeze harness and clothing (including footwear) worn only below the knee. Class rules or sailing instructions may specify a lower weight or a higher weight up to 10 kilograms. Class rules may include footwear and other clothing worn below the knee within that weight. A hiking or trapeze harness shall have positive buoyancy and shall not weigh more than 2 kilograms, except that class rules may specify a higher weight up to 4 kilograms. Weights shall be determined as required by Appendix J.

(c)   When a measurer in charge of weighing clothing and equipment believes a competitor may have broken rule 43.1(a) or rule 43.1(b) he shall report the matter in writing to the protest committee.

43.2   Rule 43.1(b) does not apply to boats required to be equipped with lifelines.

44   PENALTIES FOR BREAKING RULES OF PART 2

44.1   Taking a Penalty

A boat that may have broken a rule of Part 2 while *racing* may take a penalty at the time of the incident. Her penalty shall be a 720° Turns Penalty unless the sailing instructions specify the use of the Scoring Penalty or some other penalty. However, if she caused serious damage or gained a significant advantage in the race or series by her breach she shall retire.

44.2   720° Turns Penalty

After getting well clear of other boats as soon after the incident as possible, a boat takes a 720° Turns Penalty by promptly making two complete 360° turns (720°) in the same direction, including two tacks and two gybes. When a boat takes the penalty at or near the finishing line, she shall return completely to the course side of the line before *finishing*.

44.3   Scoring Penalty

(a)   A boat takes a Scoring Penalty by displaying a yellow flag at the first reasonable opportunity after the incident, keeping it displayed until *finishing*, and calling the race committee's attention to it at the finishing line. At that time she shall also inform the race committee of the identity of the other boat involved in the incident. If this is impracticable, she shall do so at the first reasonable opportunity within the time limit for *protests*.

(b)   If a boat displays a yellow flag, she shall also comply with the other parts of rule 44.3(a).

(c)   The boat's penalty score shall be the score for the place worse than her actual finishing place by the number of places stated in the sailing instructions, except that she shall not be scored worse than Did Not Finish. When the sailing instructions do not state the number of places, the number shall be the whole number (rounding 0.5 upward) nearest to 20% of the number of boats entered. The scores of other boats shall not be changed; therefore two boats may receive the same score.

44.4   LIMITS ON PENALTIES

(a)   When a boat intends to take a penalty as provided in rule 44.1 and in the same incident has touched a *mark*, she need not take the penalty provided in rule 31.2.

(b)   A boat that takes a penalty shall not be penalized further with respect to the same incident unless she failed to retire when rule 44.1 required her to do so.

45   HAULING OUT; MAKING FAST; ANCHORING

A boat shall be afloat and off moorings at her preparatory signal. Thereafter, she may not be hauled out or made fast except to bail out, reef sails, or make repairs. She may anchor or the crew may stand on the bottom. She shall recover the anchor before continuing in the race unless she is unable to do so.

46   PERSON IN CHARGE

A boat shall have on board a person in charge designated by the member or organization that entered the boat. See rule 75.

47   LIMITATIONS ON EQUIPMENT AND CREW

47.1   A boat shall use only the equipment on board at her preparatory signal.

47.2   No person on board shall leave, unless ill or injured or to help a person or vessel in danger. However, a person leaving the boat by accident or to swim shall be back on board before the boat continues in the race.

48   FOG SIGNALS AND LIGHTS

When safety requires, a boat shall sound fog signals and show lights as required by the International Regulations for Preventing Collisions at Sea or applicable government rules.

49   CREW POSITION

49.1   Competitors shall use no device designed to position their bodies
outboard, other than hiking straps and stiffeners worn under the thighs.

49.2   When lifelines are required by the class rules or the sailing
instructions they shall be taut, and competitors shall not position
any part of their torsos outside them, except briefly to perform a
necessary task. On boats equipped with upper and lower lifelines of
wire, a competitor sitting on the deck facing outboard with his waist
inside the lower lifeline may have the upper part of his body outside
the upper lifeline.

50   SETTING AND SHEETING SAILS

50.1   Changing Sails

When headsails or spinnakers are being changed, a replacing sail
may be fully set and trimmed before the replaced sail is lowered.
However, only one mainsail and, except when changing, only one
spinnaker shall be carried set at a time.

50.2   Spinnaker Poles, Whisker Poles

Only one spinnaker pole or whisker pole shall be used at a time except
when gybing. When in use, it shall be attached to the foremost mast.

50.3   Use of Outriggers

(a)   No sail shall be sheeted over or through an outrigger, except as
permitted in rule 50.3(b). An outrigger is any fitting or other
device so placed that it could exert outward pressure on a sheet
or sail at a point from which, with the boat upright, a vertical
line would fall outside the hull or deck planking. For the
purpose of this rule, bulwarks, rails and rubbing strakes are not
part of the hull or deck planking and the following are not
outriggers: a bowsprit used to secure the tack of a working sail,
a bumkin used to sheet the boom of a working sail, or a boom of
a boomed headsail that requires no adjustment when tacking.

(b)   (1)   Any sail may be sheeted to or led above a boom that is
              regularly used for a working sail and is permanently
              attached to the mast from which the head of the working
              sail is set.

        (2)   A headsail may be sheeted or attached at its clew to a
              spinnaker pole or whisker pole, provided that a spinnaker
              is not set.

50.4   HEADSAILS

The difference between a headsail and a spinnaker is that the mid-
girth of a headsail, measured from the mid-points of its luff and leech,
does not exceed 50% of the length of its foot, and no other
intermediate girth exceeds a percentage similarly proportional to its
distance from the head of the sail. A sail tacked down behind the
foremost mast is not a headsail.

51   MOVING BALLAST

All movable ballast shall be properly stowed, and water, dead weight
or ballast shall not be moved for the purpose of changing trim or
stability. Floorboards, bulkheads, doors, stairs and water tanks shall
be left in place and all cabin fixtures kept on board.

52   MANUAL POWER

A boat's standing rigging, running rigging, spars and movable hull
appendages shall be adjusted and operated only by manual power.

53   SKIN FRICTION

A boat shall not eject or release a substance, such as a polymer, or
have specially textured surfaces that could improve the character of
the flow of water inside the boundary layer.

54   FORESTAYS AND HEADSAIL TACKS

Forestays and headsail tacks, except those of spinnaker staysails
when the boat is not close-hauled, shall be attached approximately
on a boat's centre-line.

PART 5 – PROTESTS, HEARINGS, MISCONDUCT AND APPEALS

Section A – Protests

60 RIGHT TO PROTEST AND REQUEST REDRESS

60.1 A boat may

(a) protest another boat, but not for an alleged breach of a rule of Part 2 unless she was involved in or saw the incident; or

(b) request redress.

60.2 A race committee may

(a) protest a boat, but not as a result of a report by a competitor from another boat or other *interested party* or of information in an invalid *protest*;

(b) request the protest committee to consider giving redress; or

(c) report to the protest committee requesting action under rule 69.1(a).

60.3 A protest committee may

(a) protest a boat, but not as a result of a report by a competitor from another boat or other *interested party*, except under rule 61.1(c), nor as a result of information in an invalid *protest*;

(b) consider giving redress; or

(c) act under rule 69.1(a).

61 PROTEST REQUIREMENTS

61.1 Informing the Protestee

(a) A boat intending to protest because of an incident occurring in the racing area that she is aware of shall hail 'Protest' and conspicuously display a red flag at the first reasonable opportunity for each. She shall display the flag either until she *finishes* or retires, or, if the incident occurs near the finishing line, until the race committee acknowledges seeing her flag. In all other cases she shall inform the other boat as soon as reasonably possible.

(b)   A race committee or protest committee intending to protest a boat under rule 60.2(a) or rule 60.3(a) because of an incident it observes in the racing area shall inform her after the race within the time limit determined by rule 61.3. In all other cases it shall inform her as soon as reasonably possible.

(c)   During the hearing of a valid *protest*, if the protest committee decides to protest a boat that was involved in the incident but is not a *party* to that hearing, it shall inform the boat as soon as reasonably possible of its intention and of the time and place of the hearing.

61.2   Protest Contents

A *protest* shall be in writing and identify

(a)   the protestor and protestee;

(b)   the incident, including where and when it occurred;

(c)   any *rule* the protestor believes was broken; and

(d)   the name of the protestor's representative.

Provided the written *protest* identifies the incident, other details may be corrected before or during the hearing.

61.3   Protest Time Limit

A *protest* by a boat, or by the race committee or protest committee about an incident the committee observes in the racing area, shall be delivered to the race office no later than the time limit stated in the sailing instructions. If none is stated, the time limit is two hours after the last boat in the race *finishes*. Other race committee or protest committee *protests* shall be delivered to the race office within two hours after the committee receives the relevant information. The protest committee shall extend the time if there is good reason to do so.

62   REDRESS

62.1   A request for redress shall be based on a claim that a boat's finishing place in a race or series has, through no fault of her own, been made significantly worse by

(a)   an improper action or omission of the race committee or protest committee,

(b)   physical damage because of the action of a boat that was breaking a rule of Part 2 or of a vessel not *racing* that was required to keep clear,

(c)   giving help (except to herself or her crew) in compliance with rule 1.1, or

(d)   a boat against which a penalty has been imposed under rule 2 or disciplinary action has been taken under rule 69.1(b).

62.2   The request shall be made in writing within the time limit of rule 61.3 or within two hours of the relevant incident, whichever is later. No protest flag is required.

Section B – Hearings and Decisions

63   HEARINGS

63.1   Requirement for a Hearing

A boat or competitor shall not be penalized without a hearing, except as provided in rules 30.2, 30.3, 67 and A1.1. A decision on redress shall not be made without a hearing. The protest committee shall hear all *protests* that have been delivered to the race office unless it approves a protestor's request to withdraw the *protest*.

63.2   Time and Place of the Hearing

All *parties* to the hearing shall be notified of the time and place of the hearing, the *protest* or redress information shall be made available to them, and they shall be allowed reasonable time to prepare for the hearing.

63.3   Right to be Present

(a)   The *parties* to the hearing, or a representative of each, have the right to be present throughout the hearing of all the evidence. When the *protest* claims a breach of a rule of Part 2, Part 3 or Part 4, the representatives of boats shall have been on board at the time of the incident, unless there is good reason for the protest committee to rule otherwise. Any witness, other than a member of the protest committee, shall be excluded except when giving evidence.

(b)   If a *party* to the hearing does not come to the hearing, the protest committee may nevertheless decide the *protest*. If the *party* was unavoidably absent, the committee may reopen the hearing.

63.4   Interested Party

A member of a protest committee who is an *interested party* shall not take any further part in the hearing but may appear as a witness. A *party* to the hearing who believes a member of the protest committee is an *interested party* shall object as soon as possible.

63.5   Validity of the Protest

At the beginning of the hearing the protest committee shall decide whether all requirements for the *protest* have been met, after first taking any evidence it considers necessary. If all requirements have been met, the *protest* is valid and the hearing shall be continued. If not, it shall be closed.

63.6   Taking Evidence and Finding Facts

The protest committee shall take the evidence of the *parties* to the hearing and of their witnesses and other evidence it considers necessary. A member of the protest committee who saw the incident may give evidence. A *party* to the hearing may question any person who gives evidence. The committee shall then find the facts and base its decision on them.

63.7   Protests Between Boats in Different Races

A *protest* between boats sailing in different races conducted by different organizing authorities shall be heard by a protest committee acceptable to those authorities.

64   PROTEST DECISIONS

64.1   Penalties and Exoneration

(a)   When the protest committee decides that a boat that is a *party* to the hearing has broken a *rule*, she shall be disqualified unless some other penalty applies. A penalty shall be imposed whether or not the applicable *rule* was mentioned in the *protest*.

(b)   When as a consequence of breaking a *rule* a boat has compelled another boat to break a *rule*, rule 64.1(a) does not apply to the other boat and she shall be exonerated.

(c)   If a boat has broken a *rule* when not *racing*, her penalty shall apply to the race sailed nearest in time to that of the incident.

64.2   Decisions on Redress

When the protest committee decides that a boat is entitled to redress under rule 62, it shall make as fair an arrangement as possible for all boats affected, whether or not they asked for redress. This may be to adjust the scoring (see rule A4 for some examples) or finishing times of boats, to *abandon* the race, to let the results stand or to make some other arrangement. When in doubt about the facts or probable results of any arrangement for the race or series, especially before *abandoning* the race, the protest committee shall take evidence from appropriate sources.

64.3   Decisions on Measurement Protests

(a)   When the protest committee finds that deviations in excess of tolerances specified in the class rules were caused by damage or normal wear and do not improve the performance of the boat, it shall not penalize her. However, the boat shall not *race* again until the deviations have been corrected, except when the protest committee decides there is or has been no reasonable opportunity to do so.

(b)   When the protest committee is in doubt about the meaning of a measurement rule, it shall refer its questions, together with the relevant facts, to an authority responsible for interpreting the rule. In making its decision, the committee shall be bound by the reply of the authority.

(c)   When a boat disqualified under a measurement rule states in writing that she intends to appeal, she may compete in subsequent races without changes to the boat, but will be disqualified if she fails to appeal or the appeal is decided against her.

(d)   Measurement costs arising from a *protest* involving a measurement rule shall be paid by the unsuccessful *party* unless the protest committee decides otherwise.

65   INFORMING THE PARTIES AND OTHERS

65.1   After making its decision, the protest committee shall promptly inform the *parties* to the hearing of the facts found, the applicable *rules*, the decision, the reasons for it, and any penalties imposed or redress given.

65.2   A *party* to the hearing is entitled to receive the above information in writing, provided she asks for it in writing from the protest committee within seven days of being informed of the decision. The committee shall then promptly provide the information, including, when relevant, a diagram of the incident prepared or endorsed by the committee.

65.3   When the protest committee penalizes a boat under a measurement rule, it shall send the above information to the relevant measurement authorities.

66   REOPENING A HEARING

The protest committee may reopen a hearing when it decides that it may have made a significant error, or when significant new evidence becomes available within a reasonable time. It shall reopen a hearing when required by the national authority under rule F5. A *party* to the hearing may ask for a reopening no later than 24 hours after being informed of the decision. When a hearing is reopened, a majority of the members of the protest committee shall, if possible, be members of the original protest committee.

67   RULE 42 AND HEARING REQUIREMENT

When so stated in the sailing instructions, the protest committee may penalize without a hearing a boat that has broken rule 42, provided that a member of the committee or its designated observer has seen the incident. A boat so penalized shall be informed by notification in the race results.

† **68   DAMAGES**

The question of damages arising from a breach of any *rule* shall be governed by the prescriptions, if any, of the national authority.

Section C – Gross Misconduct

69   ALLEGATIONS OF GROSS MISCONDUCT

69.1   Action by a Protest Committee

(a)   When a protest committee, from its own observation or a report received, believes that a competitor may have committed a gross breach of a *rule* or of good manners or sportsmanship, or may have brought the sport into disrepute, it may call a hearing. The protest committee shall promptly inform the competitor in writing of the alleged misconduct and of the time and place of the hearing.

(b)   A protest committee of at least three members shall conduct the hearing, following rules 63.2, 63.3, 63.4 and 63.6. If it decides that the competitor committed the alleged misconduct it shall either

    (1)   warn the competitor or

    (2)   impose a penalty by excluding the competitor, and a boat when appropriate, from a race, or the remaining races of a series or the entire series, or by taking other action within its jurisdiction.

(c)   The protest committee shall promptly report a penalty, but not a warning, to the national authorities of the venue, of the competitor and of the boat owner.

(d)   If the competitor has left the venue and cannot be notified or fails to attend the hearing, the protest committee shall collect all available evidence and, when the allegation seems justified, make a report to the relevant national authorities.

(e)   When the protest committee has left the event and a report alleging misconduct is received, the race committee or organizing authority may appoint a new protest committee to proceed under this rule.

† **69.2   Action by a National Authority**

(a)   When a national authority receives a report required in rule 69.1(c) or rule 69.1(d), or a report alleging a gross breach of a *rule* or of good manners or sportsmanship or conduct that brought the sport into disrepute, it may conduct an investigation and, when appropriate, shall conduct a hearing. It may then take any disciplinary action within its jurisdiction it considers appropriate against the competitor or boat, or other person involved, including suspending eligibility, permanently or for a specified period of time, to compete in any event held within its jurisdiction, and suspending ISAF eligibility under rule K3.1(a).

(b)   The national authority of a competitor shall also suspend the ISAF eligibility of the competitor as required in rule K3.1(a).

(c)   The national authority shall promptly report a suspension of eligibility under rule 69.2(a) to the ISAF, and to the national authorities of the person or the owner of the boat suspended if they are not members of the suspending national authority.

69.3   Action by the ISAF

Upon receipt of a report required by rules 69.2(c) and K4.1, the ISAF shall inform all national authorities, which may also suspend eligibility for events held within their jurisdiction. The ISAF Executive Committee shall suspend the competitor's ISAF eligibility as required in rule K3.1(a) if the competitor's national authority does not do so.

Section D – Appeals

70   RIGHT OF APPEAL AND REQUESTS FOR INTERPRETATIONS

70.1   Provided that the right of appeal has not been denied under rule 70.4, a protest committee's interpretation of a *rule* or its procedures, but not the facts in its decision, may be appealed to the national authority of the venue by

  (a)   a boat or competitor that is a *party* to a hearing, or

  (b)   a race committee that is a *party* to a hearing, provided the protest committee is a jury.

70.2   A protest committee may request confirmation or correction of its decision.

70.3   A club or other organization affiliated to a national authority may request an interpretation of the *rules*, provided no *protest* that may be appealed is involved.

† **70.4**   There shall be no appeal from the decisions of an international jury constituted in compliance with Appendix Q. Furthermore, if the notice of race and the sailing instructions so state, the right of appeal may be denied provided that

  (a)   it is essential to determine promptly the result of a race that will qualify a boat to compete in a later stage of an event or a subsequent event (a national authority may prescribe that its approval is required for such a procedure),

  (b)   a national authority so approves for a particular event open only to entrants under its own jurisdiction, or

  (c)   a national authority after consultation with the ISAF so approves for a particular event, provided the jury is constituted as required by Appendix Q, except that only two members of the jury need be International Judges.

70.5   Appeals and requests shall conform to Appendix F.

71   APPEAL DECISIONS

71.1   No *interested party* or member of the protest committee shall take any part in the discussion or decision on an appeal or a request for confirmation or correction.

71.2   The national authority may uphold, change or reverse a protest committee's decision, declare the *protest* invalid, or return the *protest* for a new hearing and decision by the same or a different protest committee.

71.3   When from the facts found by the protest committee the national authority decides that a boat that was a *party* to the hearing broke a *rule*, it shall penalize her, whether or not that boat or that *rule* was mentioned in the protest committee's decision.

71.4   The decision of the national authority shall be final. The national authority shall send its decision in writing to all *parties* to the hearing and the protest committee, who shall be bound by the decision.

PART 6
ENTRY AND QUALIFICATION

75 ENTERING A RACE

75.1 To enter a race, a boat shall comply with the requirements of the organizing authority of the race. She shall be entered by

    (a)   a member of a club or other organization affiliated to a national authority,

    (b)   such a club or organization, or

    (c)   a member of a national authority.

75.2 Competitors shall comply with Appendix K, if applicable.

76 EXCLUSION OF BOATS OR COMPETITORS

76.1 The organizing authority or the race committee may reject or cancel the entry of a boat or exclude a competitor, subject to rule 76.2, provided it does so before the start of the first race and states the reason for doing so.

76.2 At world and continental championships no entry within stated quotas shall be rejected or cancelled without first obtaining the approval of the relevant international class association (or the Offshore Racing Council) or the ISAF.

77 IDENTIFICATION ON SAILS

A boat shall comply with the requirements of Appendix H governing class insignia, national letters and numbers on sails.

† 78 COMPLIANCE WITH CLASS RULES; CERTIFICATES

78.1 A boat's owner and any other person in charge shall ensure that the boat is maintained to comply with her class rules and that her measurement or rating certificate, if any, remains valid.

78.2   When a *rule* requires a certificate to be produced before a boat *races*, and it is not produced, the boat may *race* provided that the race committee receives a statement signed by the person in charge that the valid certificate exists and that it will be given to the race committee before the end of the event. If the certificate is not received in time, the boat's scores shall be removed from the event results.

78.3   When a measurer for an event concludes that a boat does not comply with her class rules, he shall report the matter in writing to the race committee, which shall protest the boat.

79   ADVERTISING

A boat and her crew shall comply with Appendix G.

80   RESCHEDULED RACES

When a race has been rescheduled, rule 36 applies and all boats entered in the original race shall be notified and, unless disqualified under rule 30.3, be entitled to sail the rescheduled race. New entries that meet the entry requirements of the original race may be accepted at the discretion of the race committee.

PART 7 – RACE ORGANIZATION

85   GOVERNING RULES

The organizing authority, race committee and protest committee shall be governed by the *rules* in the conduct and judging of races.

86   RULE CHANGES

86.1   A racing rule may not be changed unless permitted in the rule itself or as follows:

(a)   Prescriptions of a national authority may change a racing rule, but not the Definitions; a rule in the Introduction; Sportsmanship and the Rules; Part 1, 2 or 7; rule 43.1, 43.2, 69, 70, 71, 75, 76.2 or 79; a rule of an appendix that changes one of these rules; or Appendix G, J, K, L or Q.

(b)   Sailing instructions may change a racing rule by referring specifically to it and stating the change, but not rule 76.1, Appendix F, or a rule listed in rule 86.1(a).

(c)   Class rules may change only rules 42, 49, 50, 51, 52, 53 and 54.

† 86.2   If a national authority so prescribes, these restrictions do not apply if rules are changed to develop or test proposed rules in local races. The national authority may prescribe that its approval is required for such changes.

87   ORGANIZING AUTHORITY; NOTICE OF RACE; COMMITTEE APPOINTMENTS

87.1   **Organizing Authority**

Races shall be organized by an organizing authority, which shall be

(a)   the ISAF;

(b)   a member national authority of the ISAF;

(c)   a club or other organization affiliated to a national authority;

†   (d)   a class association, either with the approval of a national authority or in conjunction with an affiliated club; or

(e)   an unaffiliated body in conjunction with an affiliated club.

87.2   Notice of Race; Committee Appointments

The organizing authority shall publish a notice of race that conforms to rule M1, appoint a race committee and, when appropriate, appoint a jury.

88   RACE COMMITTEE; SAILING INSTRUCTIONS; SCORING

88.1   Race Committee

The race committee shall conduct races as directed by the organizing authority and as required by the *rules*.

88.2   Sailing Instructions

(a)   The race committee shall publish written sailing instructions that conform to rule M2.

(b)   The sailing instructions for an international event shall include, in English, the applicable prescriptions of the national authority.

(c)   Changes to the sailing instructions shall be in writing and posted within the required time on the official notice board or, on the water, communicated to each boat before her warning signal. Oral changes may be given only on the water, and only if the procedure is stated in the sailing instructions.

88.3   Scoring

The race committee shall score a race or series as required in rule A1 and by the scoring system specified in the sailing instructions.

89   PROTEST COMMITTEE

A protest committee shall be

(a)   a committee appointed by the race committee;

(b)   a jury, which is separate from and independent of the race committee; or

(c)   an international jury meeting the requirements of Appendix Q. A national authority may prescribe that its approval is required for the appointment of international juries for races within its jurisdiction, except those of the ISAF.

APPENDIX A – SCORING

See rule 88.3.

A1 GENERAL SCORING RULES

These rules apply regardless of the scoring system in effect.

A1.1 Failure to Start or Finish

When the race committee scores a boat as failing to *start* or *finish* it need not protest her.

A1.2 Boat Retiring or Disqualified After Finishing

When a boat retires or is disqualified after *finishing*, each boat that *finished* after her shall be moved up one place.

† A1.3 Scores Not Discardable

When a scoring system provides that one or more race scores are to be discarded in calculating a boat's series score, the score for disqualification under rule 2, or rule 42 when rule 67 applies, shall not be discarded.

A1.4 Unbroken Ties

(a) When boats are tied at the end of a race, the points for the place for which the boats have tied and for the place(s) immediately below shall be added together and divided equally. Boats tied for a prize shall share it or receive equal prizes.

(b) When boats have equal scores at the end of a series and a tie is unbroken by the scoring system, the scores shall remain unchanged in the final results. Boats tied for a prize shall share it or receive equal prizes.

A1.5 Numbering of Races

Races shall be numbered sequentially in the order of completion.

A1.6   A Boat's Starting Time

The time of a boat's starting signal shall be used as her starting time.

A1.7   Scores Removed From All or Part of a Series

When a boat is penalized by having her scores removed from the results of some or all races of a series, no changes shall be made in the race scores of other boats.

A2   SCORING SYSTEMS

The Bonus Point Scoring System and the Low Point Scoring System are the systems most often used. The bonus point system gives extra points for the first six places because it is harder to sail from fourth place into third, for example, than from fourteenth place into thirteenth. It is used for many class championships. The low point system is also suitable for championships, is better for small-fleet racing and is easier to use. Both systems are primarily designed for regattas but may be adapted for other series; see rule A5.

Either system may be made applicable by stating in the sailing instructions that the bonus point or low point system of Appendix A of the racing rules will apply and including the information required in rule A2.1.

A2.1   Number of Races and Series Scores

The number of races scheduled and the number required to constitute a series shall be stated in the sailing instructions. Each boat's series score will be the total of her race scores, discarding her worst score* except when prohibited in rule A1.3. The lowest series score wins.

*More than one score may be required to be discarded or all scores may be required to be counted; in either case the sailing instructions shall so state.

A2.2   Race Scores

Each boat *starting* and *finishing* in a race, and not thereafter retiring or being disqualified, will be scored points as follows:

Finishing Place	Bonus Point System	Low Point System
First	0	1
Second	3	2
Third	5.7	3
Fourth	8	4
Fifth	10	5
Sixth	11.7	6
Seventh	13	7
Each place thereafter	Add 1 point	Add 1 point

All other boats will be scored points for the finishing place one more than the total number of boats entered in the series.

A2.3   Ties

When there is a tie in series points between two or more boats, the tie will be broken in favour of the boat with the most first places, or, if the tie remains, the most second places, or lower places if necessary, using only the scores for each boat that count for her series score.

When a tie still remains, it will be broken in favour of the boat with the best score in the last race in which the tied boats *raced* and scored differently, using only the scores for each boat that count for her series score. For these calculations, if a boat has been awarded average points that do not correspond to a place, she shall be considered to have the place closest in points to the points awarded; if a boat has tied for a place, she shall be considered to have that place.

A3   ABBREVIATIONS FOR SCORING RECORDS

These abbreviations are recommended for recording the circumstances that determine a score:

DNC	Did not come to the starting area
DNS	Did not *start*
OCS	On the course side of the starting line and failed to comply with rule 29.1 or rule 30.1
DNF	Did not *finish*
RET	Retired after *finishing*
DSQ	Disqualified
DND	Disqualification not discardable because of rule A1.3
RDG	Redress given
ZPG	Z flag penalty given

A4   REDRESS

If under rule 64.2 the protest committee decides to change a boat's score, it should consider scoring her

(a)   points equal to the average, to the nearest tenth of a point (0.05 to be rounded upward), of her points in all the races in the series except [her worst race and]* the race in question, or

(b)   points equal to the average, to the nearest tenth of a point (0.05 to be rounded upward), of her points in all the races before the race in question, or

(c)   points based on the position of the boat at the time of the incident that justified the redress.

Delete these words when all scores count for series results, or adjust when more than one race is to be discarded.

A5   WHEN A SERIES IS NOT A REGATTA

In a regatta all boats are expected to compete in all races and the difference between the number of entrants and the number of starters is usually insignificant. However, in a longer series there may be a number of boats that compete in fewer races than others, in which case the following may be substituted for the second paragraph of rule A2.2:

> Boats not so scored that came to the starting area will be scored points for the finishing place one more than the number of all boats that came to the starting area. Boats that did not come to the starting area will be scored points for the finishing place one more than the number of boats entered in the series.

APPENDIX B
SAILBOARD RACING RULES

Sailboard races shall be sailed under The Racing Rules of Sailing *as changed by this appendix.*

B1   DEFINITIONS

Add the following definitions:

Capsized   A sailboard is *capsized* when her sail or the competitor's body is in the water.

Recovering   A sailboard is *recovering* from the time her sail or, when water-starting, the competitor's body is out of the water until she has steerage way.

B2   PART 2 – WHEN BOATS MEET

B2.1   The last sentence of rule 20 is changed to: 'A sailboard moving astern shall *keep clear* of other sailboards and boats.'

B2.2   Add to Section D:

23   SAIL OUT OF THE WATER WHEN STARTING

When approaching the starting line to *start*, a sailboard shall have her sail out of the water and in a normal position, except when accidentally *capsized*.

24   RECOVERING

A sailboard *recovering* shall avoid a sailboard or boat under way.

B3   PART 3 – CONDUCT OF A RACE

Rule 31 is changed to: 'A competitor shall not hold on to a starting mark.'

B4   PART 4 – OTHER REQUIREMENTS WHEN RACING

B4.1   Rule 42 is changed to: 'A sailboard shall be propelled only by the action of the wind on the sail, by the action of the water on the hull and by the unassisted actions of the competitor.'

B4.2   Rule 43.1(a) is modified to permit a competitor to wear a   er container for holding beverages. The container shall have a capacity st of at least one litre and weigh no more than 1.5 kilograms when full.

B4.3   In rule 44.2, delete 'including two tacks and two gybes.'

B5   PART 5 – PROTESTS, HEARINGS, MISCONDUCT AND APPEALS

Rule 61.1(a) is changed to:

Informing the Protestee

A sailboard intending to protest because of an incident that occurs in the racing area shall inform the other sailboard by hailing 'Protest' at the first reasonable opportunity and shall inform the race committee as soon as reasonably possible after she *finishes* or retires. In all other cases she shall inform the other sailboard as soon as reasonably possible.

B6   PART 6 – ENTRY AND QUALIFICATION

Add to rule 78.1: 'When so prescribed by the national authority, a numbered and dated device on a sailboard and her daggerboard and sail shall serve as her measurement certificate.'

B7   PART 7 – RACE ORGANIZATION

In rule 88.2(c), the last sentence is changed to: 'Changes to the sailing instructions may be communicated orally, but only if the procedure is stated in the sailing instructions.'

41

B8   **APPENDIX H – IDENTIFICATION ON SAILS**

B8.1   Add to rule H1.1(a): 'The insignia shall not refer to anything other
           than the manufacturer or class and shall not consist of more than
           two letters and three numbers or an abstract design.'

B8.2   Rules H1.3(a), (c), (d) and (e) are changed to: 'The class insignia
           shall be displayed once on each side of the sail in the area above a
           line projected at right angles from a point on the luff of the sail one
           third of the distance from the head to the wishbone. The national
           letters and sail numbers shall be in the central third of the sail above
           the wishbone and clearly separated from any advertising and shall be
           placed at different heights on the two sides of the sail, those on the
           starboard side being uppermost.'

APPENDIX C
MATCH RACING RULES

Match races shall be sailed under The Racing Rules of Sailing *as changed by this appendix. Matches shall be umpired unless the notice of race and sailing instructions state otherwise.*

C1   TERMINOLOGY

'Competitor' means the skipper, team or boat as appropriate for the event. 'Flight' means two or more matches started in the same starting sequence.

C2   CHANGES TO THE DEFINITIONS AND THE RULES OF PART 2

C2.1   The definition *Finish* is changed to: 'A boat *finishes* when any part of her hull, or crew or equipment in normal position, crosses the finishing line in the direction of the course from the last *mark* after completing any penalties.'

C2.2   Rule 17.2 is deleted.

C2.3   When rule 19.1 applies, the following arm signals by the helmsman are required in addition to the hails:

    (a)   for 'Room to tack', repeatedly and clearly pointing to windward; and

    (b)   for 'You tack', repeatedly and clearly pointing at the other boat and waving to windward.

C2.4   In rule 20 the second sentence is changed to: 'A boat taking a penalty shall *keep clear* of one that is not.'

C2.5   Rule 22.1 is changed to: 'If reasonably possible, a boat not *racing* shall not interfere with a boat that is *racing* or an umpire boat.'

C2.6 Rule 22.2 is changed to: 'Except when sailing a *proper course*, a boat shall not interfere with a boat taking a penalty or sailing on another leg.'

C2.7 A new rule 22.3 is added: 'When boats in different matches meet, any change of course by either boat shall be consistent with complying with a rule and winning her own match.'

C3 RACE SIGNALS AND RELATED RULES

C3.1 Starting Signals

The signals for starting a match shall be as follows. Times shall be taken from the visual signals; the failure of a sound signal shall be disregarded. If more than one match will be sailed, the starting signal for one match shall be the warning signal for the next match.

Time in minutes	Visual signal	Sound signal	Means
10	Flag F displayed	One	Attention signal
6	Flag F removed	None	
5	Numeral pennant displayed*	One	Warning signal
4	Flag P displayed	One	Preparatory signal
2	Blue or yellow flag or both displayed**	One**	End of pre-start entry time
0	Warning and Preparatory signals removed	One	Starting signal

Within a flight, numeral pennant 1 means Match 1, pennant 2 means Match 2, etc., unless the sailing instructions state otherwise.

**These signals shall be made only if one or both boats fail to comply with rule C4.2. The flag(s) shall be displayed until the umpires have signalled a penalty or for one minute, whichever is earlier.

C3.2   Related Rules

(a)   Rule 29.1 is changed to: 'When at her starting signal any part of a boat's hull, crew or equipment is on the course side of the starting line or its extensions, the boat shall sail completely to the pre-start side of the line before *starting*.'

(b)   Rule 29.2 is changed to: 'When at her starting signal a boat becomes subject to rule C3.2(a), the race committee shall promptly display a blue or yellow flag or both with one sound signal. Each flag shall be displayed until such boats are completely on the pre-start side of the starting line or its extensions, but not later than two minutes after the starting signal.'

(c)   In Race Signals AP and N, the last sentence is changed to: 'The attention (not the warning) or other signal will be made one minute after removal.'

C3.3   Finishing Line Signals

The race signal 'Blue flag or shape' shall not be used.

C4   REQUIREMENTS BEFORE THE START

C4.1   At her preparatory signal, each boat shall be outside a line that is perpendicular to the starting line through the starting *mark* at her assigned end. In the race schedule pairing list, the boat listed on the left-hand side is assigned the port end and shall display a blue flag at her stern while *racing*. The other boat is assigned the starboard end and shall display a yellow flag at her stern while *racing*.

C4.2   Within the two-minute period following her preparatory signal, a boat shall cross and clear the starting line, the first time from the course side to the pre-start side.

C4.3   When, after one boat has *started*, the umpires are satisfied that the other boat will not *start*, they may signal the boat that did not *start* under rule C10.4 that she is disqualified and the match terminated.

C5 PROTESTS UNDER RULES OF PART 2 BETWEEN BOATS IN THE SAME MATCH

C5.1 A boat may protest the other boat in her match under a rule of Part 2, except under rule 14 when damage resulted from contact, by clearly displaying flag Y.

C5.2 After flag Y is displayed, the umpires shall decide whether to penalize either boat. They shall signal their decision by making a single long sound signal and displaying either

   (a) a green and white flag, which means 'No penalty', or

   (b) a blue or yellow flag, which means 'The identified boat shall take a penalty by complying with rule C7 and with rule C8 or rule C9.'

C5.3 The protesting boat shall remove flag Y before or as soon as possible after the umpires' signal.

C6 OTHER PROTESTS AND REQUESTS FOR REDRESS

C6.1 Protest Limitations

   (a) A boat may protest the other boat in her match by complying with the rules of Part 5, Section A, but not under a rule of Part 2, except under rule 14 when damage resulted from contact; rules 31 and 42; or rules C4, C5, C7, C8 and C9.

   (b) A boat may protest a boat in another match but only under a rule of Part 2.

   (c) A boat intending to protest shall keep her red flag displayed until she has so informed the umpires after *finishing* or retiring.

C6.2 Redress

A boat requesting redress because of circumstances that arise before she *finishes* or retires shall display a red flag at the first opportunity after she becomes aware of those circumstances, but not later than five minutes after *finishing* or retiring.

C6.3 **Protest Committee Decisions**

(a) While afloat, the protest committee may take evidence in any way it considers appropriate and may communicate its decision orally. When the protest committee decides to conduct a hearing ashore, or to reopen or resume a hearing held on the water, it shall so advise the boats and proceed under the rules of Part 5, except that rule C6.3(b) always applies.

(b) If the protest committee decides that a breach of a *rule* has had no significant effect on the outcome of the match, it may

  (1) impose a penalty of one point or part of one point,
  (2) order a resail, or
  (3) make another arrangement it decides is equitable, which may be to impose no penalty.

C7   PENALTY SYSTEMS

C7.1 **Rule Changes**

Rules 31.2 and 44 are deleted. The sailing instructions shall state either that rule C8 or that rule C9 will apply.

C7.2 **All Penalties (Immediate and Delayed)**

(a) In rule 2, a new second sentence is inserted: 'When *racing*, a boat may wait for an umpire's decision before taking a penalty.'

(b) A boat completes a leg of the course when her bow crosses the extension of the line from the previous *mark* through the *mark* she is rounding, or on the last leg when she *finishes*.

(c) A penalized boat shall not be recorded as having *finished* until she takes her penalty and then sails completely to the course side of the line and then *finishes*, unless rule C9 applies and the penalty is cancelled before or after she crosses the finishing line.

(d) A boat taking a penalty that includes a tack shall have the spinnaker head below the mainboom gooseneck from the time she passes head to wind until she is on a close-hauled course.

C8   IMMEDIATE PENALTIES

A penalized boat shall take a penalty as follows:

(a)   When signalled before *starting* or while sailing to a windward *mark*, she shall sail clear, gybe and return to a close-hauled course. She shall do so as soon as reasonably possible but not before *starting*.

(b)   When signalled while sailing to a leeward *mark* or the finishing line she shall remain on that leg, sail clear, tack and return to a downwind course. She shall do so as soon as reasonably possible unless her spinnaker head is above the main boom gooseneck; in that case she may wait until the spinnaker is lowered, and then take the penalty as soon as possible.

C9   DELAYED PENALTIES

C9.1   A penalized boat may delay taking a penalty within the limitations of rule C9.3 but shall take it as follows, and no part of it may be taken within two of her hull lengths of a rounding *mark:*

(a)   When on a leg of the course to a windward *mark*, she shall gybe and return to a close-hauled course.

(b)   When on a leg of the course to a leeward mark or the finishing line, she shall tack and return to a downwind course.

C9.2   When a boat with a delayed penalty is on a leg to a windward *mark* and gybes, or is on a leg to a leeward *mark* or the finishing line and tacks, she shall be judged to be taking a penalty.

C9.3   If a boat has one delayed penalty, she may take the penalty any time after *starting* and before *finishing*. If a boat has two delayed penalties, she shall take one of them as soon as reasonably possible, but not before *starting*.

C9.4   If a boat has one or two delayed penalties and the other boat in her match is penalized, one penalty for each boat shall be cancelled.

C9.5   If a boat has more than two delayed penalties, the umpires shall signal her disqualification under rule C10.4.

C9.6   The umpire boat for each match shall display coloured shapes, each shape indicating one delayed penalty. When a boat has taken a penalty, or a penalty has been cancelled, one shape shall be removed. Failure of the umpires to display or remove shapes shall not change the number of penalties. The umpires shall make a short sound signal when a boat has taken a penalty.

C10   PENALTIES INITIATED BY UMPIRES

C10.1   **Rule Changes**

   (a)   Rules 60.2(a) and 60.3(a) do not apply to *rules* for which penalties may be imposed by umpires.

   (b)   Rule 64.1(b) is changed so that the provision for exonerating a boat may be applied by the umpires without a hearing, and it takes precedence over any conflicting rule of this appendix.

C10.2   When the umpires decide that a boat has broken rules 31, 42, C4, C5, C7, C8 or C9, she shall be penalized by signalling her under rule C5.2(b).

C10.3   When the umpires decide that a boat has

   (a)   failed to comply with rules C7, C8 or C9; or

   (b)   gained an advantage by breaking a *rule* after allowing for a penalty; or

   (c)   deliberately broken a *rule*; or

   (d)   committed a breach of sportsmanship;

   she shall be penalized under rule C5.2(b) or rule C10.4.

C10.4   When the umpires display a black flag and a boat's identification flag, it means: 'The signalled boat is disqualified, and the match is terminated and awarded to the other boat.'

C10.5   If umpires or protest committee members decide that a boat may have broken a *rule* other than a rule of Part 2, except rule 14 when damage resulted from contact, or a rule for which a penalty is provided in rule C10.2 or C10.3, they shall so inform the protest committee for its action under rule 60.3 and rule C6.3 when appropriate.

C11   REQUESTS FOR REDRESS OR REOPENINGS; APPEALS; OTHER PROCEEDINGS

C11.1   There shall be no request for redress or an appeal from a decision made under rule C5, C6, C7.2, C8, C9 or C10. In rule 66 the third sentence is changed to: 'A *party* to the hearing may not ask for a reopening.'

C11.2   A competitor may not base a request for redress on a claim that an action by an official boat was improper. The protest committee may decide to consider giving redress in such circumstances but only if it believes that the official boat, including an umpire boat, may have seriously interfered with a competing boat.

C11.3   No proceedings of any kind may be taken in relation to any action or non-action by the umpires.

C12   SCORING

C12.1   The winning competitor of each match scores one point (half of one point each for a dead heat); the loser scores no points.

C12.2   When a competitor withdraws from part of an event the results of all completed races shall stand.

C12.3   When multiple round robins are terminated with an incomplete round robin, only one point shall be available for all the matches sailed between any two competitors, as follows:

Number of matches completed between any two competitors	*Points for each win*
1	One point
2	One-half point
3	One-third point
(etc.)	

C12.4   In a round-robin series,

   (a)   the highest total score wins;

   (b)   a competitor who has won a match but is disqualified for breaking a rule against a competitor in another match shall lose the point for that match (but the losing competitor shall not be awarded the point); and

   (c)   the overall position between competitors who have sailed in different groups shall be decided by the total number of wins.

C12.5   In a knock-out series the sailing instructions shall prescribe the minimum number of points required to win a series between two competitors.

C13   TIES

C13.1   General

Ties shall be decided only if a sail-off is not practicable and only if necessary to determine which competitors qualify to compete in a later stage of the event or in a subsequent event. If ties remain, any monetary prizes or ranking points for tied places shall be added together and divided equally among the tied competitors.

C13.2   Round-Robin Series

   (a)   Ties between two or more competitors in a round-robin series shall be decided in favour of the competitor who has the most points in the matches between the tied competitors.

   (b)   When the tie remains, it shall be decided in favour of the competitor who has won the match against the competitor (excluding the tied competitors) who has the highest score in the round robin or, if necessary, the second highest score, and so forth until the tie is broken. When the tie is partially resolved, paragraph (a) shall be re-applied to the competitors still tied.

   (c)   When the tie remains and there have been either fleet races or previous round robins, the tie shall be resolved in favour of the competitor who has won the match against the competitor (excluding the tied competitors) who has the highest score in

51

the most recent series or, if necessary, the second-highest score, and so forth until the tie is broken. When the tie still remains it shall be decided by means of a draw.

(d) Ties from applying rule C12.4(c) shall be decided in favour of the competitor with the highest place in the different groups irrespective of the number of competitors in each group. Remaining ties shall be decided under rule C13.1.

C13.3 Knock-Out Series

(a) When a decisive match cannot be sailed to resolve a tie, including those with 0-0 scores, the tie shall be broken in favour of the competitor placed highest in the most recent round robin or the combined points from a multiple round robin.

(b) If paragraph (a) does not resolve the tie, it shall be broken in favour of the winner of the last match completed between the tied competitors unless there is a 0-0 tie. In that case a draw shall be used.

(c) Competitors eliminated in one round of a knock-out series shall be scored as tied unless more matches are sailed to break such ties.

Note: A Standard Notice of Race and Standard Sailing Instructions for match racing are available from the ISAF.

APPENDIX D – TEAM RACING RULES

Team races shall be sailed under The Racing Rules of Sailing *as changed by this appendix. If umpires or observers will be used the sailing instructions shall so state.*

D1   CHANGES TO THE RACING RULES

D1.1   The following rules are changed or added:

(a)   Add to rule 16: 'Furthermore, when boats are on a beat to windward and a *port-tack* boat is *keeping clear* of a *starboard-tack* boat, the *starboard-tack* boat shall not change course if that immediately compels the *port-tack* boat to change course.'

(b)   Add to rule 18.4: 'This rule applies only if the inside boat established the *overlap* from *clear astern*.'

(c)   Add new rule 22.3: 'Except when sailing a *proper course*, a boat shall not interfere with a boat on another leg or lap.'

(d)   Add to rule 41: 'A boat that receives help from a team-mate does not break this rule.'

(e)   If the sailing instructions so state, rule 17.2 is changed to: 'Except on a beat to windward, while a boat is less than two of her hull lengths from a *leeward* boat, she shall not sail below her *proper course* unless she gybes.'

D1.2   The following additional rules apply:

(a)   When boats in different races meet, any change of course by a boat shall be consistent with complying with a rule and winning her own race.

(b)   Right of way may be waived between team-mates provided that doing so does not directly affect a boat of the other team adversely.

(c)   A boat damaged by a team-mate boat is not eligible for redress based on that damage.

D2   INTENTION TO PROTEST; ACKNOWLEDGEMENT OF BREACHES OF RULES

D2.1   GENERAL

(a)   A boat intending to protest shall hail the other boat immediately and promptly display a red flag.

(b)   A boat that, while *racing*, may have broken a rule of Part 2, except rule 14, or rule D1 may take a penalty as provided by rules 44.1 and 44.2, except that only one turn is required. When an incident occurs at the finishing line or when an umpire's penalty is signalled at or beyond the finishing line, a boat shall not be recorded as having *finished* until she has completed her penalty and returned completely to the course side of the line before *finishing*.

(c)   When after displaying a red flag a boat is satisfied that the other boat has taken a penalty in compliance with rule D2.1(b) she shall remove her red flag.

†   (d)   The sailing instructions may state that rule D2.3(g) applies to all *protests*.

D2.2   Races Without Umpires or Observers

A boat that has displayed a red flag and then decides reasonably promptly that she, and not the other boat, was at fault shall immediately remove her flag, take a penalty in compliance with rule D2.1(b), and hail the other boat accordingly.

D2.3   Umpired Races

Races to be umpired shall be identified either in the sailing instructions or by the display of flag U no later than the warning signal.

(a)   When a boat protests under a rule of Part 2, except rule 14, or under rule D1, 31.1, 42 or 44, she is not entitled to a hearing. Instead, when the protested boat fails either to acknowledge breaking a *rule* or to take a penalty, the protesting boat may display a yellow flag and request a decision by hailing 'Umpire'.

(b)   An umpire shall signal the decision as follows:

(1)   a green flag means 'No penalty imposed; incident closed';

       (2)   a red flag means 'One or more boats are penalized.' The umpire shall hail or signal to identify each boat to be penalized. The protesting boat shall then remove her flag.

(c)   A boat penalized by an umpire's decision shall make two 360° turns (720°) in compliance with rule 44.2 as changed by this appendix.

(d)   When a boat has gained an advantage by breaking a *rule* or fails to take a penalty when required, an umpire may impose one or more additional 360° turn penalties by hailing her accordingly, or report the incident as provided in rule D2.3(e).

(e)   When an incident involves reckless sailing, rule 14, or failure to comply with an umpire's decision, the umpire may report the incident to a protest committee which may further penalize the boat concerned. The umpire shall signal this intention by displaying a black flag and hailing appropriately.

(f)   Rules 60.2 and 60.3 do not apply. The protest committee may call a hearing only on receipt of a report from an umpire as provided in rule D2.3(e) or under rule 69.

(g)   *Protests* need not be in writing, and the protest committee may take evidence in any way it considers appropriate and communicate its decision orally.

(h)   There shall be no requests for redress or to reopen a hearing or appeals by a boat arising from decisions or actions or non-actions by the umpires. The protest committee may decide to consider giving redress when it believes that an official boat may have seriously interfered with a competing boat.

D2.4   **Races with Observers**

Observers may be appointed by the race committee to observe the racing and give opinions on incidents when requested. If so, rule D2.3 applies except that

(a)   a boat need not request an opinion or accept one, in which case any *protest* shall comply with and be decided under the rules of Part 5 as changed by this Appendix;

(b)   an observer may display a yellow flag to signal that he has no opinion. If a boat then intends to protest she may do so by complying with the rules of Part 5 as changed by this Appendix.

D3   SCORING A RACE

D3.1   Each boat completing a race, whether or not rules 28.1 and 29.1 have been complied with, shall be scored points equal to her finishing place. All other boats shall be scored points equal to the number of boats entitled to *race*. In addition, a boat's score shall be increased for

	Rule broken	*Penalty points*
(a)	rule 14, 28.1 or 29.1	10
(b)	any other rule for which a penalty has not been taken under rule D2.1(b) or D2.3(c)	6

The protest committee may further increase a boat's score when it finds that she gained an advantage from breaking a *rule*. The team with the lowest total points wins. If there is a tie on points, the team having the combination of race scores that does not include a first place wins.

D3.2   When all boats of one team have *finished* or retired, the race committee may stop the race. The other team's boats shall be scored the points they would have received had they *finished*.

D3.3   When all the boats of a team fail to *start* in a race, each shall receive points equal to the number of boats entitled to *race*, and the boats of the other team shall be scored as if they had *finished* in the best positions.

D4   SCORING A SERIES

D4.1   A team racing series shall consist of races or matches. A match shall consist of two races between the same two teams. The team with the lower total points for the race or the match wins.

D4.2   When two or more teams are competing in a series consisting of races or matches, the series winner shall be the team winning the greatest number of races or matches. The other teams shall be ranked in order of number of wins. Tied matches shall count as half a win to each team.

D4.3   When necessary, ties in a series shall be broken by using, in order of precedence,

(a)   the total points scored in the series;

(b)   the points scored when the tied teams met;

(c)   if two teams remain tied after a series of matches, the last race between the teams;

(d)   unless otherwise stated in the sailing instructions, a game of chance.

D5   BREAKDOWNS WHEN BOATS ARE SUPPLIED BY THE ORGANIZING AUTHORITY

D5.1   A boat suffering a breakdown shall display a red flag as soon as practicable and, if possible, continue *racing*.

D5.2   When the race committee decides that the boat's finishing position was made significantly worse, that the breakdown was not the fault of the crew, and that in the same circumstances a reasonably competent crew would not have been able to avoid the breakdown, it shall make as equitable a decision as possible, which may be to order the race to be resailed or, when the boat's finishing position was predictable, award her points for that position. In case of doubt about her position when she broke down, the doubt shall be resolved against her.

D5.3   A breakdown caused by defective equipment or a breach of a *rule* by an opponent shall not normally be determined to be the fault of the crew, but one caused by careless handling, capsizing or a breach by a boat of the same team shall be. Any doubt about the fault of the crew shall be resolved in the boat's favour.

APPENDIX E – RADIO-CONTROLLED BOAT RACING RULES

Races for radio-controlled boats shall be sailed under The Racing Rules of Sailing *as changed by this appendix.*

E1 TERMINOLOGY

'Boat' means a boat that is radio-controlled by a competitor who is not on board. For 'race' used as a noun outside this appendix read 'heat'. Within this appendix, a race consists of one or more heats, and is completed when the last heat in the race is finished. 'Event' means one or more races. 'Series' means a specified number of races or events.

E2 PART 1 – FUNDAMENTAL RULES

E2.1 Personal Buoyancy

Add to rule 1.2: 'When on board a rescue vessel, each competitor shall be responsible for wearing personal buoyancy adequate for the conditions.'

E2.2 Aerials

Transmitter aerial extremities shall be adequately protected.

E3 PART 2 – WHEN BOATS MEET

In rule 18, change *'two-length zone'* to *'four-length zone'* and in the definition *Two-Length Zone* change *'two'* to *'four'*.

E4 PART 3 – CONDUCT OF A RACE

E4.1 Race Observers

The race committee may appoint race observers, who may be competitors. They shall hail and repeat the identity of the boats in an incident involving contact between boats or between a boat and a *mark*. Observers shall report all unresolved incidents to the race committee at the end of the heat.

E4.2   Course Board

Rule M2.1(3) is deleted. A course board showing the course and the limits of the control area shall be located next to or within the control area so as to be clearly visible to competitors *racing*.

E4.3   Control Area

Competitors *racing* and race observers shall remain in the designated control area while a heat is in progress, except that competitors may be briefly absent to perform functions permitted in rule E4.4. Competitors not *racing* shall remain outside the control area except when offering assistance under rule E5.2 or when acting as race observers.

E4.4   Launching and Re-launching

Rule 45 is changed to

(a)   Boats scheduled to *race* in a heat may be launched, taken ashore or re-launched at any time during the heat except between the preparatory and starting signals.

(b)   While ashore or at the water's edge, boats may be adjusted, drained of water or repaired; have their sails changed or reefed; have entangled objects removed; or have batteries changed.

E4.5   E4.5   Non-Applicable rules

Rules 25, 26, 30 and 33 do not apply.

E4.6   Audible Starting Signals

Audible signals for starting a heat shall be at one-minute intervals and shall be a warning signal, a preparatory signal and a starting signal. During the minute before the starting signal, verbal signals shall be made at ten-second intervals, and during the final ten seconds at one-second intervals. The start shall be at the beginning of the starting signal.

E4.7   Other Race Committee Actions

Rules 27 and 32 are changed in that the race committee shall not *postpone* or *abandon* a race before or after the start because of

(a)   foul weather, except for thunderstorms, or

(b)   insufficient wind.

E4.8   Starting and Finishing Lines

The starting and finishing lines shall be tangential to, and on the course side of, the starting and finishing *marks*.

E4.9   Individual Recall

Rule 29.2 is changed. Delete all after 'the race committee shall promptly' and insert 'twice hail "Recall, boat numbers . . .".'

E4.10   General Recall

Rule 29.3 is changed. Delete all after 'the race committee may' and substitute: 'twice hail "General recall".' The preparatory signal for a new start shall be made at least one minute after the recalled start.

E4.11   Time to Repair

Unless she has been disqualified under rule 14, a boat that has sustained damage while having right of way shall be given reasonable time, but not more than 30 minutes, to effect repairs before her next heat.

E5   PART 4 – OTHER REQUIREMENTS WHEN RACING

E5.1   Rules 43, 46, 47, 48, 49, 50, 52 and 54 do not apply.

E5.2   Outside Help

Rule 41 is changed to:

(a)   A boat that has gone ashore or aground or become entangled with another boat or object may be freed and relaunched with outside help to the extent permitted in rule E4.4.

(b)   Other actions permitted in rule E4.4 may be performed by outside help.

(c)   A competitor shall not give tactical or strategic advice to a competitor who is *racing*.

E5.3   Penalties for Breaking a Rule of Part 2, E4 or E5

(a)   Throughout rule 44 the penalty shall be one 360° turn, including one tack and one gybe, and rule 44.3 is deleted.

(b)   The race committee or protest committee may protest a boat whose competitor breaks rule E4.3, E4.4 or E5.2(c). If the protest committee decides that a *rule* was broken, it may either exclude the boat from the next race or disqualify her from the previous race.

E5.4   Ballast

Rule 51 is changed to:

During an event and unless class rules conflict,

(a)   ballast shall not be shifted, shipped, or un-shipped;

(b)   except for replacements of similar weight and position, no control equipment shall be shifted, shipped or un-shipped;

(c)   the position of counterweights may be adjusted;

(d)   bilge water shall not be used to trim the boat and may be removed at any time.

E5.5   Radio

Competitors' radio transmissions shall not interfere with the radio reception of other boats.

E5.6   Boat out of Radio Control

A competitor who loses radio control of a boat shall promptly hail and repeat 'Out of control' and the boat's sail number. A boat out of control shall retire and shall be considered an *obstruction*.

E6   PROTESTS, HEARINGS, MISCONDUCT AND APPEALS

E6.1   Protests

Add to rule 60.1: 'except that a *protest* shall be made only by a boat scheduled to race in the heat in which the incident occurred.' Add to rules 60.2(a) and 60.3(a): 'provided that during a heat, the incident is observed by a member of the race committee or protest committee within the control area.'

E6.2   Protest Requirements

Rule 61.1(a) is changed to: 'A boat intending to protest another boat because of an incident that occurs in the racing area shall twice hail "Protest" and the other boat's sail number.'

E6.3   Protest Time Limit

Rule 61.3 is changed. For 'two hours' read '15 minutes.' Add: 'A protestor intending to submit a *protest* shall inform the race committee within five minutes of the end of the relevant heat.'

E6.4   Accepting Responsibility

A boat that acknowledges breaking a rule of Part 2, 3 or 4 before a hearing may retire from the relevant heat without further penalty.

E6.5   REDRESS

(a)   Add to rule 62.1:

　　(e)   radio interference, or
　　(f)   an entanglement with a boat required to *keep clear* or *give room*.

(b)   Rule 62.2 is changed to: 'The request shall be made in writing within the time limit of rule E6.3. No protest flag is required.'

E6.6

Rule 63.3 is changed. Delete 'on board' and substitute 'within the control area'.

E6.7   Taking Evidence and Finding Facts

Add to rule 63.6: 'Evidence about an alleged breach of a rule of Part 2, 3 or 4 shall be accepted only from a witness who was within the control area at the time of the alleged incident.'

E6.8   Reopening a Hearing

Rule 66 is changed; for '24 hours' read 'five minutes'.

E6.9   Identification on Sails

Rule 77 is changed to: 'An International Class boat shall comply with the requirements of the Sail Identification Mark Rules of the Radio Sailing Division of the ISAF.'

APPENDIX F
APPEALS PROCEDURES

See rule 70. A national authority may change this appendix by prescription but it shall not be changed by sailing instructions.

F1   NATIONAL AUTHORITY

Appeals, requests by protest committees for confirmation or correction of decisions, and requests for the interpretation of *rules* shall be made to the national authority.

F2   APPELLANT'S RESPONSIBILITIES

† **F2.1**   Within 15 days of receiving the protest committee's written decision or its decision not to reopen a hearing, the appellant shall send a dated appeal to the national authority with a copy of the protest committee's decision. The appeal shall state why the appellant believes the protest committee's interpretation of a *rule* or its procedures were incorrect.

F2.2   The appellant shall also send, with the appeal or as soon as possible thereafter, any of the following documents that are available to her:

(a)   the written *protest(s)*;

(b)   a diagram, prepared or endorsed by the protest committee, showing the positions and tracks of all boats involved, the course to the next *mark* and its required side, the force and direction of the wind, and, if relevant, the depth of water and direction and speed of any current;

(c)   the notice of race, the sailing instructions, any other conditions governing the event, and any changes to them;

(d)   any additional relevant documents; and

(e)   the names and addresses of all *parties* to the hearing and the protest committee chairman.

F2.3 A request from a protest committee for confirmation or correction of its decision shall include the decision and all relevant documents. A request for a *rule* interpretation shall include assumed facts.

F3 NOTIFICATION AND RESPONSE OF THE PROTEST COMMITTEE

Upon receipt of an appeal, the national authority shall send a copy of the appeal to the protest committee, asking the protest committee for the documents listed in rule F2.2 not supplied by the appellant, and the protest committee shall send the documents to the national authority.

F4 NATIONAL AUTHORITY'S RESPONSIBILITIES

The national authority shall send copies of the appeal and the protest committee's decision to the other *parties* to the hearing. It shall send to the appellant copies of documents not sent by the appellant. It shall send to any *party* to the hearing upon request any of the documents listed in rule F2.2.

F5 ADDITIONAL INFORMATION

The national authority shall accept the protest committee's finding of facts except when it decides they are inadequate, in which case it may require the protest committee to provide additional facts or other information, or to reopen the hearing and report any new finding of facts.

F6 COMMENTS

Parties to the hearing and the protest committee may send comments on the appeal to the national authority, provided they do so within 15 days of receiving the appeal. The national authority shall send such comments to all *parties* to the hearing and to the protest committee.

F7 WITHDRAWING AN APPEAL

An appellant may withdraw an appeal before it is decided by accepting the protest committee's decision.

APPENDIX G – ADVERTISING

See rule 79. This appendix shall not be changed by sailing instructions or prescriptions of national authorities. When governmental requirements conflict with parts of it, those requirements apply.

G1 DEFINITION OF ADVERTISING

For the purposes of this appendix, advertising is the name, logo, slogan, description, depiction, a variation or distortion thereof, or any other form of communication that promotes an organization, person, product, service, brand or idea so as to call attention to it or to persuade persons or organizations to buy, approve or otherwise support it.

G2 GENERAL

G2.1 Advertisements and anything advertised shall meet generally accepted moral and ethical standards.

G2.2 This appendix shall apply when *racing* and, in addition, unless otherwise stated in the notice of race, from 0700 on the first race day of a regatta until the expiry of the time limit for lodging *protests* following the last race of the regatta.

G2.3 An event shall be designated Category A, B or C in its notice of race and sailing instructions, but if not so designated it shall be Category A. However, at the world and continental championships of Olympic classes, Category B advertising shall be permitted on hulls and, for Olympic sailboard classes, on hulls and sails. After the notice of race has been published, the category shall not be changed within ninety days before the event without prior approval of the national authority of the organizing authority.

G2.4 A national authority, or a class or the Offshore Racing Council for its events, may prescribe *rules* for advertising that are more restrictive than those of a category. For a particular event, the notice of race and the sailing instructions may include *rules* for advertising that are more restrictive than those of the event's category.

G2.5   Advertisements on sails shall be clearly separated from national letters and sail numbers.

G2.6   When, after finding the facts, a protest committee decides that a boat or her crew has broken a rule of this appendix, it shall

   (a)   warn the boat that another breach of the rule will result in disqualification; or

   (b)   disqualify the boat in accordance with rule 64.1; or

   (c)   disqualify the boat from more than one race or from the series when it decides that the breach warrants a stronger penalty; or

   (d)   act under rule 69.1 when it decides that there may have been a gross breach.

G2.7   The ISAF, a national authority, a class association or the ORC may, for its events, subject to rule G5, designate the category and may require a fee for doing so.

G2.8   The ISAF or a national authority may, for its events, prescribe *rules* and require a fee for giving consent to individual boats for advertisements, provided that such consents do not conflict with, when relevant, class rules or the rules of the ORC.

G3   CATEGORY A

G3.1   Advertising on boats other than sailboards is permitted only as follows:

   (a)   The boat's class insignia may be displayed on her sails as required by Appendix H.

   (b)   One sailmaker's mark, which may include the name or mark of the sailcloth manufacturer and the pattern or model of the sail, may be displayed on both sides of any sail and shall fit within a 150 mm x 150 mm square. On sails other than spinnakers, no part of such mark shall be placed farther from the tack than the greater of 300 mm or 15% of the length of the foot.

   (c)   One builder's mark, which may include the name or mark of the designer, may be placed on the hull, and one maker's mark may be displayed on spars and on each side of small equipment. Such marks shall fit within a 150mm x 150mm square.

(d)   The boat's type may be displayed on each side of her hull.
      Lettering shall not be higher than 1% or longer than 5% of the
      hull length of the boat, to a maximum of 100mm or 700mm
      respectively.

(e)   Makers' marks may be displayed on clothing and equipment.
      Other advertising may be displayed on clothing and equipment
      ashore.

(f)   The organizing authority of a sponsored event may permit or
      require the display of an advertisement of the event sponsor not
      larger than $0.27m^2$ in the form of a flag, and/or of a decal or
      sticker attached to each side of the hull or to a dodger on each
      side of the boat. In addition, when a sponsor supplies all hulls
      and sails at no cost to the organizing authority or competitors,
      one advertisement not larger than $0.27m^2$ may be displayed on
      each side of the mainsail. For an event of a class association or
      the ORC, such advertising requires approval by the class
      association or the ORC and, when it so prescribes, by the
      national authority concerned. Notice of such permission or
      requirement shall be included in the notice of race and the
      sailing instructions.

G3.2   Advertising on sailboards is permitted only as follows:

(a)   The sailboard's class insignia may be displayed on her sail as
      required by Appendix H.

(b)   One sailmaker's mark, which may include the name or mark of
      the sailcloth manufacturer and the pattern or model of the sail,
      may be displayed on both sides of the sail. No part of such
      mark shall be placed farther from the tack than 20% of the length of
      the foot of the sail, including the mast sleeve. The mark may
      also be displayed on the lower half of the part of the sail above
      the wishbone but no part of it shall be farther than 500mm
      from the clew.

(c)   The sailboard's type or manufacturer's name or logo may be
      placed on the hull in two places and on the upper third of the
      part of the sail above the wishbone. One maker's mark may be
      displayed on spars, on each side of small equipment and on a
      competitor's clothing and harness.

(d)   The organizing authority of a sponsored event may permit or require the display of an advertisement of the event sponsor on both sides of the sail between the sail numbers and the wishbone and on a bib worn by the competitor. For an event of a class association, such advertising requires approval by the class association and, when it so prescribes, by the national authority concerned. Notice of such permission or requirement shall be included in the notice of race and the sailing instructions.

G4   CATEGORY B

G4.1   A boat competing in a Category B event may display advertising only as permitted for Category A and by rule G4.2 (for boats other than sailboards) or rule G4.3 (for sailboards) and throughout that event shall not display advertising chosen by the boat of more than two organizations or persons. A Category B advertisement shall be either one or two of

(a)   the name of an organization or person,

(b)   a brand or product name, or

(c)   a logo.

G4.2   Advertising on Boats Other Than Sailboards

(a)   The forward 25% of each side of the hull may display no more than two advertisements chosen by the ISAF, the national authority, the class association or the ORC, for its event; or by the organizing authority of the event when it wishes to display advertising of an event sponsor. When both the organizing authority and one of the other organizations wish to use the space, they shall each be entitled to half the length of the space on each side. The remaining length of the hull shall be free of any advertising except for that permitted in rule G3.1(c) and except that half that length may be used for advertising chosen by the boat. If advertising is not displayed on the sides of the hull, it may be displayed on each side of the cabin, the insides of the cockpit coamings or sidetanks, subject to the same length dimensions.

(b)   Advertising chosen by the boat may be displayed on sails as follows:

   (1)   Advertising on spinnakers is without restriction except as provided in rules G2.5 and G4.

   (2)   On one other sail, only one advertisement may be carried at a time, and it may be on both sides of the sail. It shall be placed below the national letters and sail numbers and have a width no greater than two-thirds of the length of the foot of the sail and a height no greater than one-third of that width.

(c)   Advertising chosen by the boat may be displayed on the mainmast and main boom, but both displays shall be limited to the name, brand or product name, or logo of one organization. The space within one-third of the length of the mast and two-thirds of the length of the boom may be used.

(d)   In addition to the advertisements carried on the boat, advertisements limited to the organization(s) advertising on the boat and one or two additional organizations may be displayed on clothing and equipment worn by competitors.

G4.3   Advertising on Sailboards

(a)   The forward 25% of the hull may display no more than two advertisements chosen by the ISAF, the national authority or the class association, for its event; or by the organizing authority of the event when it wishes to display advertising of an event sponsor. When both the organizing authority and one of the other organizations wish to use the space, they shall each be entitled to half the length of the space on each side. Advertising chosen by the competitor may be displayed within the remaining length of the hull.

(b)   That part of the sail below the wishbone not used for Category A advertising may display advertising chosen by the competitor.

(c)   In addition to the advertisements carried on the sailboard, advertisements limited to the organization(s) advertising on the sailboard and one or two additional organizations may be displayed on clothing and equipment worn by competitors.

† **G5   CATEGORY C ADVERTISING**

G5.1   Approval of Advertising

Advertising for a Category C event (any event that permits advertising beyond Category B advertising) shall be

(a)   approved by the national authority of the venue unless the event is an international event;

(b)   approved by the International Sailing Federation (ISAF) when the event is an international event (i.e., an event open to entries other than those from the national authority of the venue).

G5.2   Advertising Fees

(a)   National events: The national authority of the venue may require an advertising fee for approval of Category C advertising to be paid to it.

(b)   International events: The ISAF will require an advertising fee for approval of Category C advertising, and will share the fee equally with the national authority of the venue.

G5.3   Approval Fees

The organizing authority of an event with cash or cashable prizes or appearance payments totalling more than US $10,000 or the equivalent may be required to pay an approval fee. For a national event the national authority of the venue may require such a fee to be paid to it. For an international event the ISAF will require such a fee to be paid to it.

G5.4   Rules for Category C advertising shall be stated in the notice of race and the sailing instructions

APPENDIX H
IDENTIFICATION ON SAILS

See rule 77.

† H1   ISAF INTERNATIONAL CLASS BOATS

H1.1   Identification

Every boat of an ISAF International Class or Recognized Class shall carry on her mainsail and, as provided in rules H1.3(d) and (e) for letters and numbers only, on her spinnaker and headsail

(a)   the insignia denoting her class;

(b)   national letters denoting her national authority from the table below. Except in an international championship, such letters need not be carried in home waters, nor are they required on boats of a class that uses a sequential international numbering system; and

(c)   a sail number of no more than four digits allotted by her national authority or, when so required by the class rules, by the international class association. Alternatively, if permitted in the class rules, an owner may be allotted a personal sail number by the relevant issuing authority, which may be used on all his boats in that class.

Sails measured before 31 March 1997 shall comply with rule H1.1 or with the rules applicable at the time of measurement.

Letters	*National authority*	*Letters*	*National authority*
AHO	Netherlands Antilles	ARM	Armenia
ALG	Algeria	ARU	Aruba
AND	Andorra	ASA	American Samoa
ANG	Angola	AUS	Australia
ANT	Antigua	AUT	Austria
ARG	Argentina	BAH	Bahamas

BAR	Barbados	IRL	Ireland
BEL	Belgium	ISL	Iceland
BER	Bermuda	ISR	Israel
BLR	Belarus	ISV	US Virgin Islands
BRA	Brazil	ITA	Italy
BRN	Bahrain	JAM	Jamaica
BRU	Brunei Darussalam	JPN	Japan
BUL	Bulgaria	KAZ	Kazakhstan
CAN	Canada	KEN	Kenya
CAY	Grand Cayman	KGZ	Kyrghyzstan
CHI	Chile	KOR	Korea
CHN	China	KUW	Kuwait
CIV	Ivory Coast	LAT	Latvia
COK	Cook Islands	LCA	St. Lucia
COL	Colombia	LIB	Lebanon
CRC	Costa Rica	LIE	Liechtenstein
CRO	Croatia	LTU	Lithuania
CUB	Cuba	LUX	Luxembourg
CYP	Cyprus	MAL	Malaysia
CZE	Czech Republic	MAR	Morocco
DEN	Denmark	MEX	Mexico
DJI	Djibouti	MLT	Malta
DOM	Dominican Republic	MON	Monaco
ECU	Ecuador	MRI	Mauritius
EGY	Egypt	MYA	Myanmar
ESA	El Salvador	NAM	Namibia
ESP	Spain	NED	Holland
EST	Estonia	NOR	Norway
FIJ	Fiji	NZL	New Zealand
FIN	Finland	PAK	Pakistan
FRA	France	PAR	Paraguay
GAB	Gabon	PER	Peru
GBR	United Kingdom	PHI	Philippines
GEO	Georgia	PNG	Papua New Guinea
GER	Germany	POL	Poland
GRE	Greece	POR	Portugal
GUA	Guatemala	PRK	Korea, DPR
GUM	Guam	PUR	Puerto Rico
HKG	Hong Kong	QAT	Qatar
HUN	Hungary	ROM	Romania
INA	Indonesia	RSA	South Africa, Republic of
IND	India	RUS	Russia

SEY	Seychelles	TRI	Trinidad & Tobago
SIN	Singapore	TUN	Tunisia
SLO	Slovenia	TUR	Turkey
SMR	San Marino	UAE	United Arab Emirates
SRI	Sri Lanka	UKR	Ukraine
SUD	Sudan	URU	Uruguay
SUI	Switzerland	USA	United States
SVK	Slovak Republic		of America
SWE	Sweden	UZB	Uzbekistan
TAH	Tahiti	VEN	Venezuela
THA	Thailand	YUG	Yugoslavia
TPE	Chinese Taipei	ZIM	Zimbabwe

H1.2   Specifications

(a)   National letters and sail numbers shall be in capital letters and Arabic numerals, clearly legible and of the same colour. Commercially available typefaces giving the same or better legibility than Helvetica are acceptable.

(b)   The sizes of characters and minimum space between adjoining characters on the same and opposite sides of the sail shall be related to the boat's overall length as follows:

Overall length	Minimum height	Minimum space between letters or edge of sail
Under 3.5 m	230 mm	45 mm
3.5 m–8.5 m	300 mm	60 mm
8.5 m–11 m	375 mm	75 mm
Over 11 m	450 mm	90 mm

H1.3 **Positioning**

Class insignia, national letters and sail numbers shall be positioned as follows:

(a) Except as provided in (d) and (e) below, class insignia, national letters and sail numbers shall when possible be wholly above an arc whose centre is the head point and whose radius is 60% of the leech length. They shall be placed at different heights on the two sides of the sail, those on the starboard side being uppermost.

(b) The class insignia shall be placed above the national letters. If the class insignia is of such a design that two of them coincide when placed back to back on both sides of the sail, they may be so placed.

(c) National letters shall be placed above the sail number.

(d) The national letters and sail number shall be displayed on the front side of a spinnaker but may be placed on both sides. They shall be displayed wholly below an arc whose centre is the head point and whose radius is 40% of the foot median and, when possible, wholly above an arc whose radius is 60% of the foot median.

(e) The national letters and sail number shall be displayed on both sides of a headsail whose clew can extend behind the mast 30% or more of the mainsail foot length. They shall be displayed wholly below an arc whose centre is the head point and whose radius is half the luff length and, if possible, wholly above an arc whose radius is 75% of the luff length.

† **H2** **OTHER BOATS**

Other boats shall comply with the rules of their national authority or class association in regard to the allotment, carrying and size of insignia, letters and numbers. Such rules shall, when practicable, conform to the above requirements.

H3 **CHARTERED OR LOANED BOATS**

When so stated in the notice of race or sailing instructions, a boat chartered or loaned for an event may carry national letters or a sail number in contravention of her class rules.

H4   WARNINGS AND PENALTIES

When a protest committee finds that a boat has broken a rule of this appendix it shall either warn her and give her time to comply or penalize her.

H5   CHANGES BY CLASS RULES

ISAF classes may change the rules of this appendix provided the changes have first been approved by the ISAF.

APPENDIX J – WEIGHING CLOTHING AND EQUIPMENT

See rule 43.1(b). This appendix shall not be changed by sailing instructions or prescriptions of national authorities.

J1   The items of a competitor's clothing and equipment to be weighed shall be arranged on a rack and thoroughly soaked by total immersion in water for one minute or longer if necessary for total saturation. After being soaked, the items shall be allowed to drain freely for one minute before they are weighed. Life-jackets shall be included, but not a hiking or trapeze harness or clothing worn only below the knee unless class rules require that it be included. The rack must allow the items to hang as they would hang from clothes hangers, so as to allow the water to drain freely. Hiking or trapeze harnesses shall be weighed separately and tested for positive buoyancy.

J2   During the weighing, pockets that have drainholes that cannot be closed shall be empty, but pockets or items of equipment that hold water shall be full.

J3   When a weight recorded exceeds the amount permitted, the competitor may twice rearrange the clothing and equipment on the rack and the measurer shall again soak and weigh it. If a lower weight is recorded that record shall be final.

J4   A competitor wearing a dry-suit may choose an alternative means of weighing:

       (a)   the dry-suit and items of clothing and equipment that are worn outside the dry-suit shall be weighed as described above;

       (b)   clothing worn underneath the dry-suit shall be weighed as worn while *racing*, without draining; and

       (c)   the two weights shall be added together.

APPENDIX K
COMPETITORS' ISAF ELIGIBILITY

See rule 75.2. This appendix shall not be changed by sailing instructions or prescriptions of national authorities.

K1 ISAF ELIGIBILITY RULES

To be eligible to compete in an event listed in rule K2.1, a competitor shall

(a) be governed by the regulations and rules of the ISAF;

(b) be a member of a member national authority or one of its affiliated organizations. Such membership shall be established by the competitor

    (1) being entered by the national authority of the country of which the competitor is a national or ordinarily a resident; or

    (2) presenting a valid membership card or certificate, or other satisfactory evidence of identity and membership;

(c) not be under suspension of ISAF eligibility.

K2 EVENTS REQUIRING ISAF ELIGIBILITY

K2.1 ISAF eligibility is required for the following events:

(a) the sailing regatta of the Olympic Games;

(b) the sailing regattas of regional games recognized by the International Olympic Committee;

(c) events including 'ISAF' in their titles;

(d) world and continental championships of ISAF international classes and of the Offshore Racing Council; and

(e) any other event approved by the ISAF as a world championship and so stated in the notice of race and the sailing instructions.

K2.2 ISAF eligibility may be required for any other event when so stated in the notice of race and the sailing instructions with specific reference to this appendix.

K3 SUSPENSION OF ISAF ELIGIBILITY

K3.1 After proper inquiry by either the national authority of the competitor or the ISAF Executive Committee, a competitor's ISAF eligibility shall be promptly suspended with immediate effect, permanently or for a specified period of time

(a) for any suspension of eligibility in accordance with rule 69.2; or

(b) for breaking rule 5; or

(c) for competing, within the two years preceding the inquiry, in an event that the competitor knew or should have known was a prohibited event.

K3.2 A prohibited event is an event

(a) permitting or requiring advertising beyond that permitted for Category B under Appendix G that is not approved as required by that appendix;

(b) in which cash or cashable prizes and/or appearance payments totalling more than US $10,000 (or its equivalent) may be received by any one boat, that is not approved by the national authority of the venue or, for events conducted in more than one country, the ISAF; or

(c) that is described as a world championship, either in the title of the event or otherwise, and that is not approved by the ISAF. (ISAF approval is not required for world championships of ISAF international classes or of the Offshore Racing Council.)

K3.3 When an event described in rule K3.2 has been approved as required, that fact shall be stated in the notice of race and the sailing instructions.

K4   REPORTS; REVIEWS; NOTIFICATION; APPEALS

K4.1   When a national authority suspends a competitor's ISAF eligibility under rule K3.1, it shall promptly report the suspension and reasons therefor to the ISAF. The ISAF Executive Committee may revise or annul the suspension with immediate effect. The ISAF shall promptly report any suspension of a competitor's eligibility, or of its revision or annulment by the ISAF Executive Committee, to all national authorities, international class associations, the Offshore Racing Council and other ISAF affiliated organizations, which may also suspend eligibility for events held within their jurisdiction.

K4.2   A competitor whose suspension of ISAF eligibility has been either imposed by a national authority, or imposed or revised by the ISAF Executive Committee, shall be advised of the right to appeal to the ISAF Review Board and be provided with a copy of the Review Board Rules of Procedure.

K4.3   A national authority or the ISAF Executive Committee may ask for a review of its decision by the ISAF Review Board by complying with the Review Board Rules of Procedure.

K4.4   The Review Board Rules of Procedure shall govern all appeals and requests for review.

K4.5   Upon an appeal or request for review, the ISAF Review Board may confirm, revise or annul a suspension of eligibility, or require a hearing or rehearing by the suspending authority.

K4.6   Decisions of the Review Board are not subject to appeal.

K4.7   The ISAF shall promptly notify all national authorities, international class associations and the Offshore Racing Council of all Review Board decisions.

K5   REINSTATEMENT OF ISAF ELIGIBILITY

The ISAF Review Board may reinstate the ISAF eligibility of a competitor who

(a)   applies for reinstatement;

(b)   establishes substantial, changed circumstances justifying reinstatement; and

(c)   has completed a minimum of three years of suspension.

APPENDIX L
BANNED SUBSTANCES
AND BANNED METHODS

See rule 5. This appendix shall not be changed by sailing instructions or prescriptions of national authorities. When governmental requirements conflict with parts of it, those requirements apply.

INTRODUCTION

Doping is the taking or using by a competitor of a substance or a method banned by the ISAF. Doping is governed by rule 5, this appendix, and the ISAF *Medical Lists* (containing the official lists of doping classes and methods, medicines that may be taken, and laboratories accredited for doping control) and *Doping Control Procedures* (the medical procedures leaflet). These publications, doping control forms and the ISAF schedule of penalties are available from the ISAF to national authorities and competitors on request.

L1   GENERAL

L1.1   No testing shall be initiated by the organizing authority of an event without the written authority of the ISAF or the national authority having jurisdiction over the event, except that at an event for an Olympic class it may be initiated by the national authority of the competitor to be tested.

L1.2`   A competitor selected for testing shall not refuse to be tested and shall appear at a control centre when required by a sampling officer.

L2   INITIATION OF DOPING CONTROL

The ISAF or a national authority may at any time initiate medical testing to control doping within its own jurisdiction or for competitors under its jurisdiction. A sampling officer shall be appointed to administer or supervise the testing.

L3   SELECTION

L3.1   At an authorized event, the chairman of the protest committee shall select the finishing places of competitors to be tested on the day. This may be by means of a draw or by other means decided by the protest committee. When there is more than one competitor in each boat, any or all of them may be selected. The race committee shall give to the sampling officer the names of the competitors who *finished* in the selected places. When, for any reason, no boats have *finished* in the selected places, names may be selected by means of a draw. A competitor may be tested more than once during an event.

L3.2   When the ISAF or the national authority of a competitor under its jurisdiction initiates out-of-competition testing of a competitor, it shall test only after receiving written consent from the competitor. Any such testing shall take place within the period specified in the consent.

L4   PROCEDURE

L4.1   (a)   The sampling officer or his representative shall inform a competitor by written notice, in confidence, that he or she has been selected for testing and is required to provide a urine sample at the time and place specified in the notice. The notice shall also specify the name of the sampling officer appointed for the event and of the designated laboratory to which specimens will be sent.

(b)   The competitor shall acknowledge receipt of the notice, and the time of its delivery shall be recorded by the sampling officer or his representative.

(c)   The competitor may be accompanied by one person of his or her choice.

(d)   The *Medical Lists* and *Doping Control Procedures* shall be available to the competitor on request.

(e)   A competitor who fails to appear at the appointed time and place or who refuses to provide a sample shall be removed, together with the boat in which he or she was sailing, from the event and all its results. The protest committee shall call a hearing in accordance with the rules of Part 5, Section B, to investigate the circumstances and report its findings to the ISAF or to the initiating national authority, and to the national authority of the competitor.

L4.2 The sampling officer and other persons involved in doping control shall act in accordance with *Doping Control Procedures* and shall explain all procedures for doping control to the competitor.

L4.3 The competitor shall be given a copy of the doping control form and shall sign it to acknowledge that he or she has been informed of the procedures.

L4.4 The competitor shall provide a postal or fax address at which, during the 60 days following the testing, he or she may be informed of the result of the test of sample B (rule L5).

L4.5 Failure by a competitor to acknowledge receipt of the notice (rule L4.1(b)), to sign the form (rule L4.3) or to provide an address will not be grounds for cancelling any penalty imposed for breaking rule 5.

L5   SAMPLING AND RESULTS

L5.1 The competitor shall provide a urine sample which will be divided into two samples, A and B, and sent to a designated laboratory.

L5.2 When sample A is negative, the sampling officer shall so inform the competitor immediately and no further action shall be taken.

L5.3 When sample A is positive

(a) the initiating authority shall so inform the competitor and his or her national authority immediately. No race results shall be changed at this stage; and

(b) the laboratory will proceed to test sample B. The competitor or his or her representative may be present at the testing.

L5.4 (a) When sample B is negative, the initiating authority shall so inform the competitor and his or her national authority, and no further action shall be taken.

(b)   When no result has been obtained from sample B after 60 days from the date of the testing, the test shall be considered void and no further action shall be taken.

L5.5   When sample B is positive, the ISAF or the initiating national authority will inform the competitor in writing at the address provided (rule L4.4) and his or her national authority. The ISAF will inform the national authority having jurisdiction over the event.

L5.6   (a)   Any positive result of a medical test shall be reported promptly by the initiating national authority to the ISAF.

(b)   Any penalties imposed by the national authority for breaches of rule 5 or rule L1.2 shall be reported promptly to the ISAF.

L6   APPEAL PROCEDURE

L6.1   The competitor has 20 days from the date of the communication required in rule L5.5 to appeal to the International Medical Commission (IMC) of the ISAF. When after 20 days the competitor has not appealed, his or her national authority and that of the event will be notified of this fact.

L6.2   After the last day for submitting an appeal, penalties will be applied and the scores of the competitor and the boat in which he or she was sailing shall be removed from the results of the event.

L7   EXEMPTIONS

L7.1   A competitor may ask, only in writing, for prior approval from the IMC for the use of a banned substance or a banned method for special medical reasons. The reasons shall be stated and supported with medical evidence from a doctor.

L7.2   In offshore races of more than 50 nautical miles, the use during the race of any banned substance or banned procedure for emergency medical treatment shall be reported promptly to the protest committee, which shall inform the appropriate national authority and the ISAF. The IMC may retroactively approve such use.

L8   SUSPENSION OF ISAF ELIGIBILITY

L8.1   In addition to any penalty imposed under rule K3.1, a competitor who has broken rule 5 may have his or her ISAF eligibility suspended as provided in Appendix K.

L8.2   The competitor may appeal as provided in Appendix K.

L9   COMPETITOR'S EXPENSES

Any expenses incurred in connection with this appendix by a competitor shall be his or her responsibility.

APPENDIX M – NOTICE OF RACE AND SAILING INSTRUCTIONS

See rules 87.2 and 88.2(a). The term 'race' includes a regatta or other series of races.

M1 NOTICE OF RACE CONTENTS

M1.1 The notice of race shall include the following information:

(1) the title, place and dates of the race and name of the organizing authority;

(2) that the race will be governed by *The Racing Rules of Sailing*, the prescriptions of the national authority when they apply, the rules of each class concerned, the sailing instructions and any other applicable *rules*;

(3) the classes to race, conditions of entry and any restrictions on entries;

(4) the times of registration and warning signals for the practice race or first race, and succeeding races if known.

M1.2 The notice of race shall, when appropriate, also include the following:

(1) ISAF approval and eligibility requirements (see Appendix K);

(2) the category of the event (see rule G2.3) and, when relevant, the additional information required by Appendix G;

(3) the procedure for advance registration or entry, including fees and any closing dates;

(4) an entry form, to be signed by the boat's owner or owner's representative, containing words such as: 'I agree to be bound by *The Racing Rules of Sailing* and by all other rules that govern this event';

(5) measurement procedures or requirements for measurement or rating certificates;

(6)   the time and place at which the sailing instructions will be available;

(7)   any changes to the racing rules (see rule 86);

(8)   changes to class rules, referring specifically to each rule and stating the change;

(9)   the courses to be sailed;

(10) penalties for breaking a *rule*;

(11) denial of the right of appeal, subject to rule 70.4;

(12) the scoring system;

(13) prizes, including any cash, cashable prize and/or appearance payments totalling more than US $10,000 that may be received by any one boat.

M2   SAILING INSTRUCTION CONTENTS

M2.1 The sailing instructions shall include the following information:

(1)   that the race will be governed by *The Racing Rules of Sailing*, the prescriptions of the national authority when they apply (for international events, a copy in English of such prescriptions shall be included in the sailing instructions), the rules of each class concerned, the sailing instructions and any other applicable *rules*;

(2)   the schedule of races, the classes to race and times of warning signals for each class;

(3)   the course(s) to be sailed, or a list of *marks* from which the course will be selected and, if relevant, how courses will be signalled;

(4)   descriptions of *marks*, including starting and finishing *marks*, stating the order and side on which each is to be left;

(5)   descriptions of the starting and finishing lines, the starting system and any special signals to be used;

(6)   the time limit, if any, for *finishing*;

(7)   the scoring system, stated in full or included by reference to Appendix A, class rules or other *rules* governing the event.

M2.2   The sailing instructions shall, when appropriate, also include the following:

(1)   ISAF approval and eligibility requirements (see Appendix K);

(2)   the category of the event (see rule G2.3) and, when relevant, the additional information required by Appendix G;

(3)   replacement of the relevant rules of Part 2 with the International Regulations for Preventing Collisions at Sea or other government right-of-way rules, the time(s) or place(s) they will apply, and any night signals to be used by the race committee;

(4)   changes to the racing rules permitted in rule 86, referring specifically to each rule and stating the change;

(5)   changes to class rules, referring specifically to each rule and stating the change;

(6)   restrictions controlling changes to boats when supplied by the organizing authority;

(7)   the registration procedure;

(8)   measurement or inspection procedure;

(9)   location(s) of official notice board(s);

(10) procedure for changing the sailing instructions;

(11) safety requirements, such as requirements and signals for personal buoyancy, check-in at the starting area, and check-out and check-in ashore;

(12) declaration requirements;

(13) signals to be made ashore and location of signal station(s);

(14) the racing area (a chart is recommended);

(15) approximate course length and approximate length of windward legs;

(16) the time limit, if any, for boats other than the first boat to *finish*;

(17) time allowances;

(18) class flags;

(19) the location of the starting area and any applicable restrictions;

(20) any special procedures or signals for individual or general recalls;

(21) mark boats;

(22) procedure for changes of course after the start and any special signals;

(23) any special procedure for shortening the course or for *finishing* a shortened course;

(24) restrictions on use of support boats, plastic pools, radios, etc.; on hauling out; and on outside assistance provided to a boat that is not *racing*;

(25) the penalty for breaking a rule of Part 2 other than the 720° Turns Penalty;

(26) protest procedure and times and place of hearings;

(27) denial of the right of appeal, subject to rule 70.4;

(28) the national authority's approval of the appointment of an international jury under rule 89(c);

(29) substitute competitors;

(30) the minimum number of boats appearing in the starting area required for a race to be started;

(31) when and where races *postponed* or *abandoned* for the day will be resailed;

(32) tides and currents;

(33) prizes, including any cash, cashable prize and/or appearance payments totalling more than US $10,000 that may be received by any one boat;

(34) other commitments of the race committee and obligations of boats.

APPENDIX N
SAILING INSTRUCTIONS GUIDE

This guide provides a set of tested sailing instructions designed primarily for major championship regattas for one or more classes. They therefore will be particularly useful for world, continental and national championships and other events of similar importance. The guide can also be useful for other events; however, for such events some of these instructions will be unnecessary or undesirable. Race officers should therefore be careful in making their choices.

The principles on which all sailing instructions should be based are as follows:

1 They should include only two types of statement: the intentions of the race committee and the obligations of competitors.

2 They should be concerned only with racing. Information about social events, assignment of moorings, etc., should be provided separately.

3 They should not change the racing rules except when clearly desirable.

4 They should not repeat or restate any of the racing rules.

5 They should not repeat themselves.

6 They should be in chronological order; that is, the order in which the competitor will use them.

7 They should, when possible, use words or phrases from the racing rules.

To use this guide, first review rule M2, Sailing Instruction Contents. Then delete all optional instructions that will not be needed. Instructions that are required or strongly recommended are marked with an asterisk (*). Then select the paragraphs desired where more than one version is shown. Then fill in the spaces where a bullet (•) appears, following the directions in the left margin, and select the desired wording where a choice is indicated by alternatives in brackets ([____]). Finally, renumber all instructions in sequential order.

NOTE: *The notes in the left hand column contain guidance for preparing sailing
           instructions. Do not include them in the completed draft.*

*On separate lines,
insert the full name of
the regatta, the
inclusive dates from
measurement or the
practice race until the
final race, the name of
the organizing
authority, and the city
and country.*

_____

_____

_____

_____

SAILING INSTRUCTIONS

*1   Rules

*Insert the full names of
the national authority,
when applicable, and of
the class(es). Insert
the appropriate category
(see Appendix G).*

The regatta will be governed by The Racing
Rules of Sailing (RRS), the prescriptions of the ●,
the rules of the ● class(es), except as any of these
are changed by these sailing instructions, and by
these sailing instructions. The regatta is
designated Category ●.

*2   Entries

*Insert the competitor
eligibility conditions,
if any.*

*Insert the Conditions of
Entry clause as
recommended by the
RYA in Addendum C
(RYA) to this
appendix.*

Eligible boats may be entered by completing
registration with the organizing authority.
Eligibility requirements for boats are ●. Eligibility
requirements for competitors are ●.

*3   Notices to Competitors

*Insert the specific
location(s).*

Notices to competitors will be posted on the
official notice board(s) located ●.

*4   **Changes in Sailing Instructions**

Insert the times.   Any change to the sailing instructions will be
                              posted before ● on the day it will take effect, except
                              that any change to the schedule of races will be
                              posted by ● on the day before it will take effect.

·5   **Signals Made Ashore**

Insert the specific   5.1   Signals made ashore will be displayed at ●.
location.

Insert the sound signal 5.2 Flag AP with two ● (one ● when lowered) means
and time.   'The race is postponed. The warning signal will
                              be made not less than ● minutes after AP is
                              lowered.'

Insert the sound signal. 5.3 Flag B fully hoisted with one ● means 'Protest
                              Time has begun.' When lowered half way, it
                              means 'There are less than 30 minutes
                              remaining before protest time ends.' When
                              lowered, it means 'Protest Time has ended.'

*6   **Schedule of Races**

Insert the days, dates   Races are scheduled as follows:
and times. Include any
practice races.

Race	Day and date	Time of warning signal
___	_____	_____
___	_____	_____
___	_____	_____

(etc.)

Insert the time.   No warning signal will be made after ● on the
                              last day of racing.

7   **Class Flags**

Insert the class names   Class flags will be:
and names or
descriptions of flags.

Class	Flag
_____	_____
_____	_____

A section of a chart or other suitable map should be copied and marked for this purpose.

8   Racing Area

The racing area will be as shown in Illustration A, attached.

*9   The Course

Insert the distances and the number of the leeward mark. Delete the last sentence when not applicable.

Attach the course diagram(s). A method of illustrating various courses is shown in Addendum A

*9.1 The diagram(s) in Illustration B show the course(s), including the approximate angles between legs, the order in which marks are to be passed, and the side on which each mark is to be left. Mark 1 will be approximately • nautical miles from Mark •. The first and last legs will be approximately • longer than the distance from Mark • to Mark 1.

Insert the number of the leeward mark.

9.2 The approximate compass bearing from Mark • to Mark 1 will be displayed from the race committee signal boat.

Insert the number of the leeward mark. Include the gate in the diagram as shown below.

9.3 If the race committee sets a gate instead of Mark •, boats shall sail between Mark •S and Mark •P from the direction of the last mark and round either Mark •S to starboard or Mark •P to port, as shown below.

Mark ___ S   Mark ___ P

Do not use if courses may be shortened.

9.4 Courses will not be shortened. This changes rule 32.

Insert the descriptions of all marks and the instruction number. Delete any mark numbers that do not apply.

*10   Marks

Marks 1, 2, 3 and 4 will be •. New marks, as provided in instruction •, Change of Course After the Start, will be •. The starting and finishing marks will be •.

Use the last part of the sentence for a multi-class regatta. Insert the number of the system, the number of minutes and the class names in order of starting.

(This is a new starting system that the ISAF hopes will be tried.)

*11 The Start

*11.1 Races will be started using rule 26, System •, with classes starting at • minute intervals in the order •

(OR)

*11.1 Races will be started as follows. This changes rules 26.1 and 30. Times shall be taken from the visual signals; the failure of a sound signal shall be disregarded.

Title	Signals
Warning	Class flag, 1 sound
Preparatory	Blue flag or flag P, I, Z, or black flag; 1 sound
Starting	Flags removed, 1 sound

The preparatory signal will be displayed one minute after the warning signal and will be removed, with one sound, one minute before the starting signal. The starting signal will be displayed five minutes after the preparatory signal.

Succeeding classes will be started as follows:

(a) at five-minute intervals by displaying the warning and preparatory signals with the starting signal for the preceding class, or

(b) at any time after the starting signal for the preceding class by displaying the warning signal for the succeeding class.

Insert the number of
the leeward mark.

*11.2 The starting line will be between a staff displaying an orange flag or shape on the race committee boat at the starboard end and Mark • at the port end.

(OR)

*11.2 The starting line will be between a staff displaying an orange flag or shape on the race committee boat at the starboard end and the port-end starting mark.

(OR)

Delete the last sentence
when signals will be
made from the
starboard-end race
committee boat.

*11.2 The starting line will be between staffs displaying orange flags or shapes on two race committee boats. Signals will be made from a race committee signal boat stationed to windward of the line.

(OR)

*11.2 The starting line will be between staffs displaying orange flags on Starting Marks A and B and between staffs displaying orange flags on Starting Marks B and C as shown below. Mark B may not be on a straight line between Mark A and Mark C. For the purpose of rule 30.1, the extensions of the starting line are the extensions beyond Marks A and C.

Mark A •   •   • Mark C
                        Mark B

(OR)

*11.2 There will be a Gate Start, in accordance with Addendum D (RYA) of this appendix.

Use only for a multi-
class regatta. Insert
'warning' when classes
start at ten- minute
intervals, 'preparatory'
when they start at five-
minute intervals.

11.3 Boats whose • signal has not been made shall keep clear of the starting area and of all boats whose • signal has been made.

Insert the number of   **11.4**   A boat shall not start later than • minutes after
minutes.   her starting signal.

Insert the description of   **12**   **Mark Boats**
the flag or shape.

Mark boats will be stationed beyond each mark.
At the finish, the mark boat will be stationed
beyond the finishing line. When on station only,
each mark boat will display a •. Failure of a mark
boat to be on station or to display her signal will
not be grounds for redress. This changes rule
62.1(a).

13   **Change of Course After the Start**

A change of course after the start will be signalled
before the leading boat has begun the leg,
although the new mark may not then be in
position. Any mark to be rounded after rounding
the new mark may be relocated to maintain the
original course configuration. When in a
subsequent change of course a new mark is
replaced, it will be replaced with an original mark.

*14   **The Finish**

The finishing line will be between a staff displaying
an orange flag or shape on a race committee boat
and the nearby mark at the port end.

(OR)

The finishing line will be between a staff
displaying an orange flag or shape on a race
committee boat and the port-end finishing mark.

(OR)

The finishing line will be between staffs displaying
orange flags or shapes on two race committee
boats.

<table>
<tr><td>Delete if the 720°
Turns Penalty will be
used. Insert the number
of places.</td><td>15</td><td>Penalty System</td></tr>
</table>

15   Penalty System

*Delete if the 720°
Turns Penalty will be
used. Insert the number
of places.*

The Scoring Penalty, rule 44.3, will apply. The penalty will be ● places.

(OR)

the RYA Time Penalty will apply, in accordance with Addendum E (RYA) of this appendix.

*16   Time Limit

*Insert the time(s) and
class(es). Adjust for a
single class regatta or
for a single time limit
for all classes.*

The time limit will be ● for the ● class and ● for the ● class. Boats failing to finish within ● minutes after the first boat finishes or within the time limit, whichever is later, will be scored Did Not Finish. This changes rule 35.

17   Protests

Insert the time.

17.1 Protests shall be written on forms available at the race office and delivered there within ● after the time of the last boat's finish.

(OR)

Insert the times.

17.1 Protests shall be written on forms available at the race office and delivered there within Protest Time which will begin at ● and end at ●.

(OR)

17.2 Protests will be heard in approximately the order of receipt as soon as possible.

(OR)

Insert the time.

17.2 Protests will be heard in approximately the order of receipt beginning at ●.

17.3 Protest notices will be posted within 30 minutes of the protest time limit to inform competitors where and when there is a hearing in which they are parties to a hearing or named as witnesses.

Use only when the requirements of rule 70.4 are met.

17.4 Decisions of the [jury] [protest committee] will be final as provided in rule 70.4.

17.5 Rule 66 is changed by adding this sentence: 'On the last day of racing, a party to the hearing may ask for a reopening no later than one hour after being informed of the decision.'

*18 Scoring

Insert the numbers.

The [Bonus Point] [Low Point] scoring system, rule A2, will apply. • races are scheduled, of which • races shall be completed to constitute a series.

(OR)

Insert the number of races.

The [Bonus Point] [Low Point] scoring system, rule A2, will apply, modified so that each boat's series score will be the total of her race scores, with her worst score discarded if • or more races have been completed. • races are scheduled, of which • races shall be completed to constitute a series.

(OR)

Insert the name of the class and the rule number.

For the • class, the class scoring system, rule • of the class rules, will be used.

19 Support Boats

Insert 'the disqualification of ' or 'points for • additional places added to the scores of '. In the latter case insert the number of places.

Team leaders, coaches and other support personnel shall not be in the racing area from the time of the preparatory signal for the first class to start until all boats have finished or the race committee signals a postponement, general recall or abandonment. The penalty for failing to comply with this requirement will be • all boats associated with the support personnel who do so.

20   Haul-out Restrictions

When this applies to some classes only, insert the name(s) of the class(es) between 'all' and 'boats'. Insert the time. Use (b) only when there is a scheduled reserve day.

All boats shall be afloat before • on the day preceding the first scheduled race and shall not be hauled out during the regatta except:

(a)   with and according to the terms of prior written permission of the [jury] [protest committee]; or

(b)   after the race preceding a reserve day, in which case they shall again be afloat before • on the day preceding the next race.

21   Plastic Pools and Diving Equipment

Insert the class(es) and time.

Underwater breathing apparatus, plastic pools or their equivalent shall not be used around • class boats after • on the day preceding the first scheduled race.

22   Radio Communication

A boat shall neither make radio transmissions while racing nor receive radio communications not available to all boats.

23   Prizes

Change as required. When perpetual trophies are to be awarded, refer to them by their complete names. State, when appropriate, that cash or cashable prizes and/or appearance payments totalling more than US $10,000 (or its equivalent) may be received by any one boat.

Prizes will be awarded to each member of the crews placing first, second and third in the regatta.

Addendum A – Illustrating the Course

Shown here are examples of course illustrations. Any course can be similarly shown. When there is more than one course, prepare a separate diagram for each course and state how each will be signalled.

This course is frequently used. Options include
(1) varying the interior angles of the triangle (45°–90°–45° and 60°–60°–60° are common),
(2) deleting the last windward leg,
(3) using a gate instead of a leeward *mark* for downwind legs (not reaches),
(4) using an offset *mark* at the beginning of downwind legs (not reaches), and
(5) using the leeward and windward *marks* as starting and finishing *marks*. Be sure to specify the interior angle at each *mark*.

Start - 1 - 2 - 3 - 1 - 3 - Finish

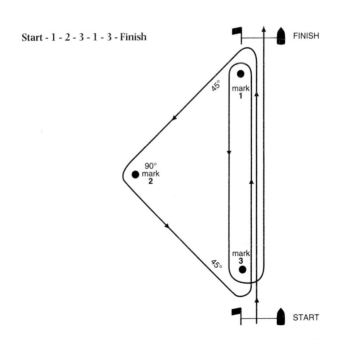

This course is frequently used. Options include
(1) increasing or decreasing the number of laps,
(2) deleting the final windward leg,
(3) using a gate instead of a leeward *mark*,
(4) using an offset *mark* at the windward *mark*, and
(5) using the leeward and windward *marks* as starting and finishing *marks*, respectively.

Start - 1 - 3 - 1 - 3 - Finish

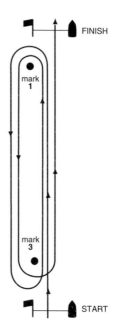

Trapezoid courses are becoming more common in multi-class regattas. Options include
(1) adding additional legs,
(2) using gates instead of leeward *marks* for downwind legs (not reaches),
(3) varying the interior angles of the reaching legs,
(4) using an offset *mark* at the beginning of downwind legs (not reaches), and

(5) finishing boats upwind rather than on a reach. Be sure to specify the interior angle of each reaching leg. It is recommended that Mark 4 be different from the starting *mark*.

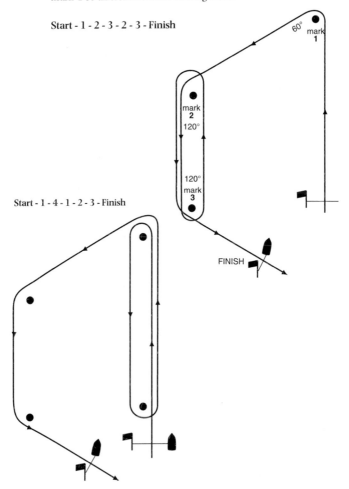

Start - 1 - 2 - 3 - 2 - 3 - Finish

Start - 1 - 4 - 1 - 2 - 3 - Finish

ADDENDUM B – BOATS PROVIDED BY THE ORGANIZING AUTHORITY

The following sailing instruction is recommended when all boats will be provided by the organizing authority. It can be added to, changed, or shortened to suit the circumstances. When used, it should be inserted following instruction 5.

6 **Boats**

6.1 Boats will be provided for all competitors, who shall not modify them or cause them to be modified in any way except that

(a) a compass may be tied or taped to the hull or spars;

(b) wind indicators, including yarn or thread, may be tied or taped anywhere on the boat;

(c) hulls, centreboards and rudders may be cleaned only with water;

(d) adhesive tape may be used anywhere above the water line; and

(e) all fittings or equipment designed to be adjusted may be adjusted, provided that the class rules are observed.

6.2 All equipment provided with the boat for sailing purposes shall be in the boat while afloat.

6.3 The penalty for not complying with one of the above rules will be disqualification from all races sailed in which the rule is broken.

6.4 Competitors shall report any damage or loss of equipment, however slight, to the organizing authority's representative immediately after securing the boat ashore. The penalty for breaking this instruction, unless the [jury] [protest committee] is satisfied that the competitor made a determined effort to comply, will be disqualification from the race most recently sailed.

Use when the regatta is not restricted to class members.

6.5 Class rules requiring competitors to be members of the class association will not apply.

ADDENDUM C (RYA)

The safety of a boat and her entire management including insurance shall be the sole responsibility of the owner person in charge who must ensure that the boat and crew are adequate to face the conditions that may arise in the course of the race. Neither these sailing instructions nor any inspection of the boat limits or reduces the absolute responsibility of the owner/person in charge for the crew, the boat and her management. The race organisers shall not be responsible for any loss, damage, death or personal injury howsoever caused to the owner/person in charge or crew, as a result of their taking part in the race or races. Moreover, every owner/person in charge warrants the suitability of the boat for the race or races.

ADDENDUM D (RYA) - GATE START

The following sailing instructions are recommended when a gate start is required.

1   When flag G is displayed on the race committee boat a gate start will be used.

2   A starting mark will be laid at the leeward end of the gate.

3   The gate launch will display flag G and the guard launch will display flag U. Starting signals will be made on the race committee boat.

4   The pathfinder for the first race will be nominated by the race committee.

Subsequently, the pathfinder will be the tenth boat in the preceding race. When she is unable to race, or has been the pathfinder previously in the event, the pathfinder will be the eleventh boat in the preceding race and so on. Her number will be posted on the official notice board. The pathfinder shall report to the gate launch five minutes before the warning signal.

5   At or around the starting signal the pathfinder will sail from the starting mark on a close-hauled port tack. During the start the pathfinder will be followed by the gate launch and the guard launch will keep station off the pathfinder's starboard bow.

6   The starting line will be between the starting mark and the stern of the gate launch.

7   The pathfinder shall maintain her course until released by the race officer.

Insert the time.   8   After the release of the pathfinder, the gate launch will maintain her course and speed until •minutes after the starting signal, When she stops she will lower flag G half way and make a sound signal.

9   A boat not having correctly started which is on the port side of the gate launch while the gate is opening, shall not cross the starting line from the course side.

10   After the preparatory signal a boat which interferes with or tries to pass between the pathfinder and the gate or guard launch, or that causes another boat to interfere in these ways, will be disqualified without a hearing. If the race is restarted, resailed or rescheduled she is not entitled to compete.

11   The gate launch, the guard launch and the pathfinder until release, rank as starting marks.

12   A boat that cannot avoid touching a starting mark may hail a right-of-way boat for room and shall retire.

Insert the time.   13   A boat shall not start later than •. minutes after the starting signal when flag G on the gate launch and the race committee boat will be lowered.

ADDENDUM E (RYA) TIME PENALTY

The RYA recommends the use of the Time Penalty when it is not practicable to use the 720° Turns Penalty, the automatic loss of places is thought to make the Scoring Penalty too severe and the elapsed times of boats is recorded. A time penalty may also be used for touching a mark when it is not practicable for a boat to perform a 360° turn [   ]. The sailing instruction may be varied to specify a different percentage, or that the percentage be added to her corrected time, or that a stated number of seconds be added to her elapsed or corrected time.

Time Penalty

Rule 44, [and rule 31.2] will not apply. A boat that may have broken a rule of Part 2 while racing [or which has broken rule 31.1] may take a Time Penalty, unless she has caused serous damage or gained a significant advantage in the race or series in which case she shall retire. The Time Penalty will be to add 1% of her elapsed time to her elapsed time, rounding the increased time to the nearest second.

Rules 44.3(a) and (b) apply, substituting Time Penalty for Scoring Penalty throughout.

Rule 44.4 is amended to read:

(a)   When a boat intends to take a Time Penalty for breaking a rule of Part 2 and in the same incident has touched a mark she need not take the penalty for breaking rule 31.1.

(b)   A boat that takes a penalty shall not be penalized further with respect to the same incident unless she failed to retire when this sailing instruction required her to do so.

(c)   A boat shall not be scored as having finished outside a time limit solely by the application of a time penalty.

APPENDIX P – RECOMMENDATIONS FOR PROTEST COMMITTEES

This appendix is advisory only; in some circumstances changing these procedures may be advisable. It is addressed primarily to protest committee chairmen but may also help judges, jury secretaries, race committees and others connected with protest hearings.

In a protest hearing, the protest committee should weigh all testimony with equal care; should recognize that honest testimony can vary, and even be in conflict, as a result of different observations and recollections; should resolve such differences as best it can; should recognize that no boat or competitor is guilty until a breach of a *rule* has been established to the satisfaction of the protest committee; and should keep an open mind until all the evidence has been heard as to whether a boat or competitor has broken a *rule*.

P1 PRELIMINARIES
(may be done by the race office staff)

- Receive the form from the protestor.

- Note on the form the time the *protest* is lodged and when protest time ends.

- Inform each *party*, and the race committee when necessary, when and where the hearing will be held.

P2 BEFORE THE HEARING

Make sure that

- each *party* has a copy of the protest form. When copies are unavailable let the protestee read the *protest* before beginning.

- no member of the protest committee is an *interested party*. Ask the *parties* whether they object to any member. .

- only one person from each boat (or *party*) is present unless an interpreter is needed.

- all boats and people involved are present. If they are not, however, the committee may proceed under rule 63.3(b).

- boat representatives were on board when required (rule 63.3(a)). When the *parties* were in different races, both organizing authorities must accept the composition of the protest committee (rule 63.7). In a measurement *protest* obtain the current class rules and identify the authority responsible for interpreting them (rule 64.3(b)).

P3 THE HEARING

P3.1 Check the validity of the *protest* or request for redress.

- Were the contents adequate (rule 61.2)?

- Was it delivered in time? If not, is there good reason to extend the time limit (rule 61.3)?

- When required, was the protestor involved in or a witness to the incident (rule 60.1(a))?

- When necessary, was 'Protest' hailed and the protest flag flown correctly (rule 61.1(a))?

- When the flag and hail were not necessary was the protestee informed?

- Decide whether the *protest* is valid (rule 63.5).

- Once the validity of the *protest* has been determined, do not let the subject be introduced again unless truly new evidence is available.

P3.2 Take the evidence (rule 63.6).

- Ask the protestor and then the protestee to tell their stories. Then allow them to question one another.

- Invite questions from protest committee members.

- Make sure you know what facts each *party* is alleging before calling any witnesses. Their stories may be different.

- Allow anyone, including a boat's crew, to give evidence. It is the *party* who must decide which witnesses to call. The question 'Would you like to hear N?' is best answered by 'It is your choice.'

- Call the protestor's and then the protestee's witnesses (and committee's if any) one by one. Limit *parties* to questioning witnesses (the parties may wander into general statements).

- Invite the protestee to question the protestor's witness first (and vice versa). This prevents the protestor from leading his witness from the beginning.

- Allow a member of the protest committee who saw the incident to give evidence (rule 63.6) but only in the presence of the *parties*. The member may be questioned and may remain in the room (rule 63.3(a)).

- Try to prevent leading questions or hearsay evidence, but if that is impossible discount the evidence so obtained.

- Only accept written evidence when both *parties* agree.

- Ask one member of the committee to note down evidence, particularly times, distances, speeds, etc.

- Invite first the protestor and then the protestee to make a final statement of her case, particularly on any application or interpretation of the *rules*.

P3.3 Find the facts (rule 63.6).

- Write down the facts; resolve doubts one way or the other.

- Call back *parties* for more questions if necessary.

- When appropriate, draw a diagram of the incident using the facts you have found.

P3.4 Decide the *protest* (rule 64).

- Base the decision on the facts found (if you cannot, find some more facts).

- In redress cases, make sure that no further evidence is needed from boats that will be affected by the decision.

P3.5 Inform the *parties* (rule 65).

- Recall the *parties* and read them the facts found and decision. When time presses it is permissible to read the decision and give the details later.

- Give any *party* a copy of the decision on request. File the protest form with the committee records.

P4   REOPENING A HEARING (Rule 66)

When a timely request is made for a hearing to be reopened, hear the *party* making the request, look at any video, etc., and decide whether there is any material new evidence which might lead you to change your decision. Decide whether your interpretation of the *rules* may have been wrong; be open-minded as to whether you have made a mistake. If none of these applies refuse to reopen; otherwise schedule a hearing.

P5   GROSS MISCONDUCT (Rule 69)

P5.1   An action under this rule is not a *protest*, but the protest committee gives its allegations in writing to the competitor before the hearing. The hearing is conducted under the same rules as other hearings but must have at least three members (rule 69.1(b)). Use the greatest care to protect the competitor's rights.

P5.2   A competitor or a boat cannot protest under rule 69, but the protest form of a competitor who tries to do so may be accepted as a report to the protest committee which can then decide whether to call a hearing or not.

P5.3   When it is desirable to call a hearing under rule 69 as a result of a Part 2 incident, it is important to hear any boat-v-boat *protest* in the normal way, deciding which boat, if any, broke which *rule*, before proceeding against the competitor under this rule.

P5.4   Although action under rule 69 is taken against a competitor, not a boat, a boat may also be penalized.

P5.5   The protest committee may warn the competitor when it believes this to be sufficient penalty, in which case no report need be made to the national authority. When the penalty is more severe and a report is made to the national authority, it is helpful to recommend to the national authority whether or not further action should be taken.

P6   APPEALS (Rule 70 and Appendix F)

When decisions can be appealed,

- leave the papers so that the information can easily be used for an appeal. Is there an adequate diagram? Are the facts found sufficient? (Example: was there an *overlap*? YES/NO. 'Perhaps' is not a fact found.) Are the names of the protest committee members on the form, etc.?

- comments on any appeal should enable the appeals committee to picture the whole incident clearly; the appeals committee knows nothing about the situation.

P7   PHOTOGRAPHIC EVIDENCE

Photographs and videos can sometimes provide useful evidence but protest committees should recognize their limitations and note the following points:

- The *party* producing the photographic evidence is responsible for arranging the viewing.

- View the tape several times to extract all the information from it.

- The depth perception of any single-lens camera is very poor; with a telephoto lens it is non-existent. When the camera views two *overlapped* boats at right angles to their course, it is impossible to assess the distance between them. When the camera views them head on, it is impossible to see whether an *overlap* exists unless it is substantial.

- Ask the following questions:

  - where was the camera in relation to the boats?
  - was the camera's platform moving? If so in what direction and how fast?
  - is the angle changing as the boats approach the critical point? Fast panning causes radical change.
  - did the camera have an unrestricted view throughout?

APPENDIX Q
INTERNATIONAL JURIES

See rules 70.4 and 89(c). This appendix shall not be changed by sailing instructions or prescriptions of national authorities.

Q1 COMPOSITION, APPOINTMENT AND ORGANIZATION

Q1.1 An international jury shall be composed of experienced sailors with excellent knowledge of the racing rules and extensive protest committee experience. It shall be independent of and have no members from the race committee, and be appointed by the organizing authority subject to approval by the national authority if required (see rule 89(c)).

Q1.2 The jury shall consist of a chairman, a vice chairman if desired, and other members for a total of at least five. A majority shall be International Judges. The jury may appoint a secretary, who shall not be a member of the jury.

Q1.3 No more than two members (three, in Group M, South and West South America; Group N, Central and East South America; or Group Q, Africa - South of the Sahara) shall be from the same national authority.

Q1.4 The jury may divide itself into two or more panels of at least five members, of which the majority shall be International Judges. If this is done, the requirements for jury membership shall apply to each panel but not to the jury as a whole.

Q1.5 When the jury has fewer than five members, because of illness or emergency, and no qualified replacements are available, it remains properly constituted if it consists of at least three members. In this case, members shall be from different national authorities except in Group M (South and West South America), Group N (Central and East South America) and Group Q (Africa-South of the Sahara), where two members may be from the same national authority.

Q1.6 When the national authority's approval is required for the appointment of an international jury (see rule 89(c)), notice of its approval shall be included in the sailing instructions or be posted on the official notice board.

Q1.7   If the jury acts while not properly constituted, the jury's decisions may be appealed.

Q2   RESPONSIBILITIES

Q2.1   An international jury is responsible for hearing and deciding all protests and other matters arising under the rules of Part 5. When asked by the organizing authority or the race committee, it shall advise and assist them on any matter directly affecting the fairness of the competition.

Q2.2   Unless the organizing authority directs otherwise, the jury shall

    (a)   decide questions of eligibility, measurement or boat certificates; and

    (b)   authorize the substitution of competitors, boats, sails or equipment.

Q2.3   If so directed by the organizing authority, the jury shall

    (a)   make or approve changes to the sailing instructions,

    (b)   supervise or direct the race committee in the conduct of the races, and

    (c)   decide on other matters referred to it by the organizing authority.

Q3   PROCEDURES

Q3.1   Decisions of the jury shall be made by a simple majority vote of all members. When there is an equal division of votes cast, the chairman of the meeting may cast an additional vote.

Q3.2   When it is considered desirable that some members not participate in discussing and deciding a protest, the jury remains properly constituted if at least three members remain.

Q3.3   Members shall not be regarded as interested parties (see rule 63.4) by reason of their nationality.

Q3.4   If a panel fails to agree on a decision it may adjourn and refer the matter to the full jury.

Time in Seconds to advance 1 length

Boat Speed Knots	Length of Yacht in Metres						
	4	5	6	7	8	9	10
1	7.8	9.8	11.8	13.7	15.9	17.6	19.6
2	3.9	4.9	5.9	6.9	7.8	8.8	9.8
3	2.6	3.3	3.9	4.6	5.2	5.9	6.5
4	2.0	2.4	2.9	3.4	3.9	4.4	4.9
5	1.4	2.0	2.4	2.7	3.1	3.5	3.9
6	1.3	1.6	2.0	2.3	2.6	3.0	3.3
7	1.1	1.4	1.7	2.0	2.2	2.5	2.8
8	1.0	1.2	1.5	1.7	2.0	2.2	2.5
9	0.9	1.1	1.3	1.5	1.7	2.0	2.2
10	0.8	1.0	1.2	1.4	1.6	1.8	2.0

$$1 \text{ knot of boat-speed} = 1.688\text{ft per sec.}$$
$$= 0.515\text{m per sec.}$$

Boat velocities for given wind speeds

This table gives approximations only. Velocities are for non-planing boats that are reaching or running. For beating, velocities will be lower, and multiplying by 0.8 will yield an approximate result.

WIND		LENGTH OF BOAT AT WATERLINE (feet)														
		10		12		14		16		18		20		25		30	
Kts	Bft	Kts	f/s	Kts	f/s	Kts	f/s	Kts	f/s	Kts	f/s	Kts	f/s	Kts	f/s	Kts	f/s
1	1	0.2	0.3	0.2	0.3	0.2	0.3	0.2	0.3	0.3	0.5	0.3	0.5	0.3	0.5	0.4	0.6
2		0.4	0.6	0.5	0.8	0.5	0.8	0.5	0.8	0.6	1.0	0.6	1.0	0.7	1.1	0.8	1.3
3		0.7	1.1	0.7	1.1	0.8	1.3	0.8	1.3	0.9	1.5	0.9	1.5	1.1	1.8	1.2	2.0
4	2	0.9	1.5	1.0	1.6	1.1	1.8	1.1	1.8	1.2	2.0	1.3	2.1	1.4	2.3	1.6	2.7
5		1.1	1.8	1.2	2.0	1.3	2.1	1.4	2.3	1.5	2.5	1.6	2.7	1.8	3.0	2.0	3.3
6		1.4	2.3	1.5	2.5	1.6	2.7	1.7	2.8	1.8	3.0	1.9	3.2	2.2	3.7	2.4	4.0
7	3	1.6	2.7	1.7	2.8	1.9	3.2	2.0	3.3	2.2	3.5	2.3	3.8	2.5	4.2	2.8	4.7
11	4	2.5	4.2	2.8	4.7	3.0	5.0	3.2	5.4	3.4	5.7	3.6	6.0	4.0	6.7	4.4	7.4
17	5	3.9	6.5	4.3	7.2	4.7	7.9	5.0	8.4	5.3	8.9	5.6	9.4	6.2	10.4	6.8	11.4
22	6	5.1	8.6	5.6	9.4	6.0	10.1	6.5	10.9	6.9	11.6	7.2	12.1	8.1	13.6	8.9	15.0

WIND		Ft. per sec.	M. per sec.	
BFT	MPH			
1	1	1.46	0.44	Light air, ripples
	2	2.93	0.88	
	3	4.39	1.32	
	4	5.86	1.76	
2	5	7.33	2.20	Light breeze, small wavelets
	6	8.79	2.64	
	7	10.26	3.08	
	8	11.73	3.52	
3	9	13.19	3.96	Gentle breeze, large wavelets
	10	14.66	4.40	
	11	16.12	4.84	
	12	17.59	5.28	
4	13	19.05	5.72	Moderate breeze, small waves, frequent white horses
	14	20.52	6.16	
	15	21.99	6.60	
	16	23.45	7.04	
5	17	24.92	7.48	Fresh breeze, moderate waves, white horses
	18	26.39	7.92	
	19	27.85	8.36	
	20	29.32	8.80	
	21	30.78	9.24	
	22	32.25	9.68	
	23	33.71	10.12	
6	24	35.18	10.56	Strong breeze, foaming crests
	25	36.65	11.00	

INDEX

References are to rules (e.g., 27.3), appendices (e.g., A1.4 or B), or sections (e.g., Introduction). Locations for sections are on the Contents page. Headings are arranged alphabetically; the references that follow them are arranged in the order in which they appear in the book. Italics are used for words that appear in Definitions. An italicized word at the end of an entry and before any subheading means that its Definitions text contains the heading word (e.g., contact: 14, C, E, keep clear). Appendices B, C, D, E, J, M, N and P are not indexed in detail.

RYA PRESCRIPTIONS

The RYA prescribes

Rule
68   Damages

1. No claim for damages arising from breaches of any of these rules or the sailing instructions shall be adjudicated upon by any race committee or appeal authority, but shall be subject to the jurisdiction of the courts.
2. A boat that acknowledges breaking a rule by retiring or taking a penalty does not thereby admit liability for damage.
3. The findings of fact and decisions of protest committees shall be relevant only to the purposes of the ISAF *Racing Rules of Sailing* and shall not be referred to in any proceedings for damages without the written consent of all parties to the protest.

69.2   Allegations of Gross Misconduct - Action by a National Authority

When the RYA Tribunal conducts a hearing in a case that has been the subject of an appeal under rule 70 and finds facts that differ from the facts found by the protest committee, the Racing Rules Committee may, if it thinks fit, reopen the appeal and reconsider its decision.

70.4   Right of Appeal

An organizing authority shall obtain approval from the RYA for the denial of appeal according to rule 70.4. The letter of approval shall be available for inspection during the event.

78   Compliance with Class Rules; Certificates

The race committee may inspect or measure any boat at any time.

86.2   Rule Changes

A race committee wishing to develop and test a rule change in its local regattas may do so but shall obtain prior approval from and report the results to the RYA.

87.1(d) Organizing Authority

An International Class Association shall obtain approval for its World or European Championship to be held within the jurisdiction of the RYA three months before issuing the Notice of Race.

89(c) Protest Committee - International Jury

An organizing authority shall obtain approval from the RYA for the constitution of an international jury. The letter of approval shall be available for inspection during the event.

APPENDIX A SCORING

A1.3 Scores not Excludable

This rule shall not apply unless the notice of race and sailing instructions state otherwise.

APPENDIX D TEAM RACING

D2.1(d) Rule D2.1(g) shall apply only when an RYA National Judge or an International Judge is appointed to chair the protest committee.

APPENDIX F   APPEALS PROCEDURE

F2.1 Rule F2.1 shall not apply. Instead, within 15 days of receiving the protest committee's written decision or its decision not to reopen a hearing, the appellant shall write to the RYA Racing Division stating an intention to lodge an appeal. No details are needed at this stage. The RYA will send the appellant an Appeal Form, which shall be completed as far as possible, to form the appeal, and returned to the RYA within 15 days together with a copy of the protest committee's decision.

If the appellant fails to meet the requirements of the appeal procedure the RYA will refuse to hear the appeal save in exceptional circumstances. If other parties to the protest or the protest committee fail to meet the requirements of the procedure the RYA may decide the appeal as it thinks fit.

APPENDIX G ADVERTISING

G5   **Category C.**

An organizing authority shall obtain approval for the adoption of Category C not less than six months before the start of the event. A fee may be required.

APPENDIX H IDENTIFICATION ON SAILS

H1   **Identification**

The requirements of rules H1.1, H1.2 and H1.3 apply to all British owned boats except that:

(a)   under rule H1.1(a), class insignia need not be carried when the boat carries a sail number from one of the series specified in 2(a), (b), (c) or (d) below.

(b)   under rule H1.1(c), a sail number of more than four digits may be carried.

(c)   under rule H1.1(c), for boats other than ISAF classes, one of the authorities specified in 2 below shall allot an appropriate sail number.

(d)   under rule H1.2(b), the height of a letter included as part of a sail number shall be the same as any numerals included in the sail number.

(e)   under rule H1.3(c), the national letters may be placed in front of or above the sail numbers.

H2   **Series of sail numbers and issuing authorities approved by the RYA**

(a)   Y,M,N,T,A and L series issued by the RYA.

(b)   R series issued by the Royal Ocean Racing Club.

(c)   C series issued by the Clyde Yacht Clubs Association.

(d)   UK IOR and IMS series issued before 1 April 1993.

(e)   National class series issued by the RYA.

(f)   Series issued by RYA affiliated class associations and approved by the RYA.

(g)   Series issued by a builder of a new class and approved by the RYA

DEFINITIONS

A term used as stated below is shown in italic type or, in preambles, in bold italic type.

Abandon A race that a race committee or protest committee *abandons* is void but may be resailed.

Clear Astern and Clear Ahead; Overlap One boat is *clear astern* of another when her hull and equipment in normal position are behind a line abeam from the aftermost point of the other boat's hull and equipment in normal position. The other boat is *clear ahead*. They *overlap* when neither is *clear astern* or when a boat between them *overlaps* both. These terms do not apply to boats on opposite *tacks* unless rule 18 applies.

Finish A boat *finishes* when any part of her hull, or crew or equipment in normal position, crosses the finishing line in the direction of the course from the last *mark* either for the first time or, if she takes a penalty, after complying with rule 31.2 or rule 44.2.

Interested Party A person who may gain or lose as a result of a protest committee's decision, or who has a close personal interest in the decision.

Keep Clear One boat *keeps clear* of another if the other can sail her course with no need to take avoiding action and, when the boats are *overlapped* on the same *tack*, if the *leeward* boat can change course in both directions without immediately making contact with the *windward* boat.

Leeward and Windward A boat's *leeward* side is the side that is or, when she is head to wind, was away from the wind. However, when sailing by the lee or directly downwind, her *leeward* side is the side on which her mainsail lies. The other side is her *windward* side. When two boats on the same *tack overlap*, the one on the *leeward side* of the other is the *leeward* boat. The other is the *windward* boat.

Mark An object the sailing instructions require a boat to pass on a specified side, excluding its anchor line and objects attached temporarily or accidentally.

Obstruction An object that a boat could not pass without changing course substantially, if she were sailing directly towards it and one of her hull lengths from it. An object that can be safely passed on only one side and an area so designated by the sailing instructions are also *obstructions*. However, a boat *racing* is not an *obstruction* to other boats unless they are required to *keep clear* of her, give her *room* or, if rule 21 applies, avoid her.

Overlap See *Clear Astern and Clear Ahead; Overlap.*